EMOTIONAL
JUSTICE

EMOTIONAL JUSTICE

*A Roadmap
for Racial Healing*

Esther A. Armah

BK°
Berrett–Koehler Publishers, Inc.

Berrett-Koehler Publishers, Inc.   Tel: (510) 817-2277
1333 Broadway, Suite 1000   Fax: (510) 817-2278
Oakland, CA 94612-1921   www.bkconnection.com

ORDERING INFORMATION

Quantity sales. Special discounts are available on quantity purchases by corporations, associations, and others. For details, contact the "Special Sales Department" at the Berrett-Koehler address above.

Individual sales. Berrett-Koehler publications are available through most bookstores. They can also be ordered directly from Berrett-Koehler: Tel: (800) 929-2929; Fax: (802) 864-7626; www.bkconnection.com.

Orders for college textbook / course adoption use. Please contact Berrett-Koehler: Tel: (800) 929-2929; Fax: (802) 864-7626.

Distributed to the U.S. trade and internationally by Penguin Random House Publisher Services.

Berrett-Koehler and the BK logo are registered trademarks of Berrett-Koehler Publishers, Inc.

Printed in the United States of America

Berrett-Koehler books are printed on long-lasting acid-free paper. When it is available, we choose paper that has been manufactured by environmentally responsible processes. These may include using trees grown in sustainable forests, incorporating recycled paper, minimizing chlorine in bleaching, or recycling the energy produced at the paper mill.

Library of Congress Cataloging-in-Publication Data

Names: Armah, Esther, author.
Title: Emotional justice : a roadmap for racial healing / Esther A. Armah.
Description: First edition. | Oakland, CA : Berrett-Koehler Publishers, [2022] | Includes index.
Identifiers: LCCN 2022014864 (print) | LCCN 2022014865 (ebook) | ISBN 9781523003365 (paperback) | ISBN 9781523003372 (pdf) | ISBN 9781523003389 (epub) | ISBN 9781523003396
Subjects: LCSH: Racial justice. | Racism. | Social justice. | Healing.
Classification: LCC HT1561 .A76 2022 (print) | LCC HT1561 (ebook) | DDC 305.8—dc23/eng/20220609
LC record available at https://lccn.loc.gov/2022014864
LC ebook record available at https://lccn.loc.gov/2022014865

First Edition

28 27 26 25 24 23 22   10 9 8 7 6 5 4 3 2 1

Cover designer: Mike Nichols. *Cover photo:* Andrea Buso.
Book design and production: Leigh McLellan Design. *Copyeditor:* Michelle Jones.
Proofreader: Joanne Farness. *Indexer:* Ken DellaPenta.

For Ma and Pa
silence breakers
independence shapers
roadmap influencers
Ma, you walk your walk in the most glorious way.
Pa, you taught me to keep company with my mind.
I feel you watch over me in quiet ways.

Contents

Foreword

Dr. Brittney Cooper

I first attended one of Esther Armah's signature conversations on racial justice at the Brecht Forum in New York City in the spring of 2012. After that first forum, I was hooked, and tried to attend every Emotional Justice conversation that she moderated thereafter. It was there in those spaces where Armah, a journalist who has worked on three continents, pushed her interlocutors to grapple with what she termed the "emotionality" of their political and personal investments. Never one for fluffy conversations about feelings when white supremacy and patriarchy are clearly about structures, I would sit riveted as her guests shared revelation after revelation about what it meant to actually begin to live out the things they believed in.

Like so many well-read, academically inclined folks, I have often used esoteric theories, argumentative premises, and heady ideas as my entry point into orienting myself in the world. This is a fancy way of saying that I hid behind big words and even bigger concepts to win political fights. These felt for me like a more steady and trustworthy compass than the mercurial emotions that I might encounter in myself or anyone else on any given day. It was in watching Armah build out her framework for Emotional Justice in real time that I began to understand where my thinking was fundamentally wrong. Anytime political arguments devolved into shouting matches, Armah helped me to see that it was never about the politics themselves. It was always about the emotional worlds in which those politics lived, always about the underlying traumas that gave birth to them.

That our politics cannot be separated from either our emotions or our traumas has been for me an earthshaking revelation. In fact, there is no contemporary thinker who has more deeply influenced how I practice my politics than Esther Armah and her Emotional Justice framework. It is no exaggeration to say that it was a decade of learning at her feet—first as a member of her audience, then as a listener to her radio programs, and then as her friend—that helped me to articulate rage as the critical emotion that powers my own investments in feminism, a discussion which I took up in my book *Eloquent Rage*. I share that simply to tell you that Esther has influenced a whole generation of writers and thinkers. Her work has offered the blueprint for how to engage our emotional lives in ways that might actually lead toward liberation. You can hear her influence even when her name has not been called.

That is why I am elated for this book. I already cherish it. I will teach it. I will read it again and again. We have ever more sophisticated analyses, beautifully written and hard-hitting, about the range of social conditions that beset us in the afterlives of European empire. In every place, those legacies are the twinned ills of slavery and colonization. Despite this accreting work, things don't seem to get better. Not for long anyway. We have better language, yet we still continue to miss the point. This is because we don't need more explications of our politics, our traumas, why Black and white folks can't get along, why Black men don't love Black women. In some ways we've heard it all before. What we need is Emotional Justice. Without it, we cannot have racial justice or gender justice or climate justice or any kind of justice. It is the emotional life of our politics with which we refuse to wrestle that kills our movements, dismantles our relationships, and diminishes our capacity for empathy.

This book is the missing puzzle piece, the one that will crack us open at the center, showing us both how much trauma is present and how deep our politics have not in fact penetrated. A daughter of Ghana by way of London, Esther Armah has lived every iteration of this afterlife, from a childhood spent in post-Independence Ghana, to a young adulthood spent in London, to nearly a decade living and working in New York City. Therefore, she lets no one off the hook. In this framework that thinks primarily about relations between white and Black folks, she calls for each demographic to do their work, to think about how we participate in the emotional perpetuation of oppressive systems, the ways our feelings keep us from doing the right thing.

Over the last decade, the Emotional Justice framework has made me a better teacher, a better writer, a better activist, and a better friend. I know it's hard to believe that one concept can do that much work, but I said what I said. Every single time I think that I just need a better thesis statement, that I just need to figure out how to win the argument, I hear Esther telling me that the argument I'm trying to win isn't about politics after all. It's about emotions. "Get to the center of those; locate the trauma," I hear her saying. And then you will get to a clearer place about how to stop harming one another. This book will call you out. Prepare yourself. It will call you in. Don't resist it. It will rearrange your whole life. And you will recognize after this that you had things out of place this whole time anyway. You will be grateful for it. I am. Eternally.

Dr. Brittney Cooper, author of the
New York Times best seller, *Eloquent Rage*

Foreword

Dr. Robin DiAngelo

I am white, and I have been engaged in educating other white people on systemic racism for over twenty years. This education requires challenging the ideologies that uphold racism, which include color blindness, meritocracy, and individualism. Yet challenging these ideologies has very real material consequences as white people react with intense emotions.

There are many reasons why white people are so defensive about the suggestion that we benefit from, and are complicit in, a racist system, including the following:

- Social taboos against talking openly about race
- The racist = bad / not racist = good binary
- Fears of people of color
- Our view of ourselves as objective individuals
- Our guilt and knowledge that there is more going on than we can or will admit to

Our emotional reactions when these norms are challenged may be automatic, but they are not *natural*. We have been deeply conditioned into them, and they function to protect the racist status quo. White emotionality is the connective tissue of systemic racism. When I first heard Esther Armah explain Emotional Justice, I knew that this was the missing piece: even though white people have the concepts, it is our emotional reactions—our false sense of scarcity and threat— that continually holds racism in place and keeps us from acting in solidarity.

We tend to see emotions as emerging unbidden from some internal and private place. And because we see emotions this way, we tend to take them at face value. Even so, not all emotions are sanctioned; the legitimacy they are granted varies based on why, when, and how they are expressed and who is expressing them. For example, white men can express anger and be seen as powerful leaders, whereas Black men expressing anger are seen as threatening. White women expressing anger are seen as shrill, whereas Black women are seen as aggressive and out of control. In other words, we are conditioned to express and interpret emotions in particular ways; they are not purely natural or unique to each individual. Emotions have social consequences, and they invoke behaviors that are then acted out and that impact others collectively. Emotional Justice reframes emotions in ways that make visible the racial and political context in which they emerge and gives us the emotional language and literacy we need if we are to end racism.

A key aspect of whiteness is that it does not require white people to develop the emotional capacity to withstand racial discomfort, and certainly not to think politically about our emotions. The result is the punitive power of white fragility, which functions as a form of social control and racial policing. White emotionality structures the everyday realities of Black people in ways that have material impacts. Emotional Justice offers white people a powerful framework through which to understand racism at the emotional level and develop the stamina to free ourselves. In so doing, Armah moves us from our heads to our hearts.

If we are to authentically challenge systemic racism, we must begin to understand the sociopolitical nature of emotions. If we could end racism from a purely intellectual place, we would have done so. In these pages, Esther Armah, with elegance and precision, offers us a way forward. *Emotional Justice* recognizes the sociopolitical dimensions of emotionality and seeks to heal the trauma that—left unaddressed—keeps us attached to white supremacy. For white people, healing this trauma entails the appropriate expression of loss, grief, and rage. These are feelings that we have either collectively sublimated or acted out as white fragility. Here, Armah illuminates how we can transform historical trauma into liberatory action, and in so doing, heal ourselves and the larger structures in which we feel and act.

Dr. Robin DiAngelo, author of the
New York Times best seller, *White Fragility*

In Need of
Emotional Justice

We are navigating a new world whose future demands global racial healing and dismantling systemic inequity. To get to that future means working through a racial reckoning. For that we need tools. All over America, all over Europe, all over the world, in communities, places of learning and labor and leadership globally, our work and our future require this combination of racial healing and dismantling systemic inequity.

We need these tools to help us listen, engage, and stay when every part of us wants to run; to seek refuge in our good intentions, our solid arguments, our progressive politics; and to deflect and deny that this is our work to do. It is no one else's. This new world does not have a shelf life; it is not a blip or a moment. It is the future we yearn for.

Until now, we have been navigating this racial healing lacking crucial understanding, and therefore lacking adequate emotional tools, deficient in effective language but wanting to be better, to do right, to harm less, to repair, to heal, to lead with love, to win.

What we need is Emotional Justice. This is a new love language for racial healing and social justice. It grapples with a legacy of untreated trauma from a history of horror and harm that has shaped, impacted, and affected all of us. I am a Black woman who built and shaped Emotional Justice over fifteen years in three cities across four countries on three continents— North America, Europe, and Africa. It has been engaged by communities of Black, Brown, and white leaders, managers, and workers who highlight how it applies to them, their journey, their community, their particularity. They come from the sectors of philanthropy, academia, activism, journalism, art, law, education, medicine. They are Black women and men, white women and men, and Brown women and men. They are leaders who built organizations; they are managers navigating the corporate world; they are activists and teachers; they are shaping the work of diversity, equity, and inclusion.

This global work of racial healing is ours to do. The work is not the same in Black and white bodies. There is the specific work for white people to do with one another; there is the work Black people need to do with one another; and there is the work between Black and white people. We all have our work to do. And Emotional Justice is fresh language that we can learn to speak and share when it comes to racial healing and dismantling systemic inequity.

We are a global family, interconnected and interdependent. Nobody wins when the family feuds. But the racial feud is centuries deep, rooted and wretched, wrapped in histories and policies of power, profit, and pain that privilege some and punish others. The umbilical cord of our humanity has been cut by white supremacy and its offspring, racism. Emotional Justice offers us a new way to bind, to heal, and to win.

It is our guide. On these pages, I share Emotional Justice and the love languages by creating a roadmap for racial healing. Let's journey together.

• 1 •

What Is
Emotional Justice?

Emotional Justice is a roadmap for racial healing, focusing on the emotional work that white, Black, and Brown people need to do to end systemic inequity. That emotional work entails exploring, identifying, and severing the connections in our relationship to power and race that uphold systemic inequity, by unlearning the language of whiteness. This relationship shapes how we lead, learn, work, see ourselves and one another as Black, Brown, Indigenous, and white people. That's because the connections are about identity, essence, emotions, intimacy, trauma, heart, and soul—not intellect, ideology, or philosophy. Emotional Justice engages and explores how a legacy of untreated trauma from global histories of injustice shapes us. It transforms how we lead, learn, work, and see ourselves and others. It is about loving one another more justly, in order to make our world more justice centered.

We have justice movements to change our world for the better—social justice, environmental justice, gender justice, labor justice. Each speaks to a particular part of the fight for our global humanity, and engages issues of injustice, inequity, or violence that threaten that humanity. Emotional Justice is part of this family. I don't treat the emotional in the purely individual sense. I treat the emotional as structural. Emotional Justice is specifically about the role emotions play when it comes to race, whiteness, power, and sustaining inequity. History and politics help us see the need for social, environmental, gender, or climate justice. Similarly, Emotional Justice explores the impact of history's systems of oppression when it comes to the emotional. Like the other justice movements, Emotional Justice connects the histories of oppression to what is happening now, what is going wrong, and how we can put it right. It connects us to the role of the emotional within systems that cause harm. Putting the two words together— *emotional* and *justice*—is about highlighting that this is our collective work, a group focus connected to institutional change. Emotional Justice joins the family of justice movements fighting to bring people together to heal a harm that impacts all of us, and to make change that benefits all of us. It is not a replacement for social or racial justice. It is a crucial untold but pivotal addition.

This roadmap for racial healing gives us fresh language we can learn to speak and share when it comes to race, racial repair, and racial healing. A roadmap has signs with information that keeps you on your path toward a specific destination. It helps ensure you're going in the right direction; it identifies location, helps you stay on track, and ensures you arrive at your chosen destination. That's what Emotional Justice does: locates where we are when it comes to the emotional regarding race, trauma, whiteness, and history. It explains how we got here, identifies the next place to go, and ensures and affirms that you are on the right path and equipped to get to the next sign. A roadmap does this with signs; Emotional

Justice does it with a love language of phrases—those we must unlearn, and those we will replace them with.

The Roadmap

Emotional Justice is about unlearning the language of whiteness and replacing it with an Emotional Justice love language. The language of whiteness is the thread stitched into the fabric of systems of oppression that build connection and sustain our relationship to power, centering whiteness. It is a narrative about who we are as white, Black, Brown, and Indigenous people and about our role in the world, with a central focus on white men. It is a false narrative that says whiteness is the world, has built the world, and saves the world.

The language of whiteness lays the foundation and is the heartbeat of sustained injustice. At its soul, that language centers a notion of supremacy and issues of dominion, subjugation, exploitation. Supremacy means being better than somebody. In order for that to be real, this language created this narrative about itself as a global savior and civilizer, with Black, Brown, and Indigenous people as savages needing saving and civilizing. No one is immune from the weight and toll of this narrative of whiteness that permeates every sector, industry, and aspect of our lives as people across all parts of the world.

We must unlearn this language. This unlearning is required of all peoples—white, Black, Brown, and Indigenous. If we do not unlearn the language of whiteness, we cannot fully dismantle systems of inequity. And if we do not dismantle them, we maintain cycles of progress and regress that exhaust, devastate, and debilitate.

The systems of oppression that built the world were about labor, race, and power. The labor was always unequal. Racial healing with Emotional Justice means that all of us are doing emotional work. There can be no Emotional Justice without the equal division of emotional labor. Dividing up that emotional labor to do the work of dismantling means naming the connections; contextualizing the relationship to the emotional, to power and whiteness; and identifying who should do what, because although we all—white, Black, Brown, Indigenous—have work to do, our work is not all the same. It is crucial that we understand this and identify who has what work to do and why it is they, and they alone, who must do that work. How do we do that? We start by identifying the four pillars of the language of whiteness. Each has a name and a definition.

The Language of Whiteness

Here are the four pillars of the language of whiteness:

* Racialized emotionality
* Emotional patriarchy
* Emotional currency
* Emotional economy

Racialized emotionality: a world where we add gender, color, context, and consequence to universal human emotions. The universal becomes racialized. The racialized is then dehumanized. The dehumanized becomes the ongoing target of violence.

Emotional patriarchy: a society that centers, privileges, and prioritizes the feelings of men, centrally white men, no matter the cost or consequence to all women and to Black, Brown, and Indigenous peoples.

Emotional currency: a society that treats women—particularly Black women—as currency that appreciates or depreciates according to its service to whiteness, men, and, centrally, white men.

Emotional economy: a world that makes decisions and creates policies that revolve around the feelings of white men, and is relentlessly driven by those feelings regardless of the harm to the health of a nation. The emotional economy functions to sow division, to plant seeds that segregate, and to spin narratives that separate.

This is what we are unlearning. We must then replace each with an Emotional Justice love language. What does that look like?

The Emotional Justice Love Languages

There are four Emotional Justice love languages. Each has a name and a definition.

- Intimate reckoning
- Intimate revolution
- Resistance negotiation
- Revolutionary black grace

Intimate reckoning: for white women and men to do the emotional labor of severing their connection to power and race that upholds a white masculinity centering the subjugation and exploitation of Black, Brown, and Indigenous people, and white women. That means to stop defending, supporting, uplifting, and cheering a white masculinity that sustains the language of whiteness and shapes white men's emotional connection to and relationship with power and race.

Intimate revolution: for Black women to sever the connection between labor, value, and worth by centering rest and replenishment. This connection stretches back into a history where labor was life and death, conditioning Black women to see their sole worth as connected to, and measured by, labor, struggle, and servitude to people outside themselves. This connection comes with a parallel narrative of laziness, gender, and race, making it complex. It is how the language of whiteness is spoken by global BIPOC women. That complexity means reimagining the relationship to labor that associates rest with guilt; it means normalizing rest and severing a connection to labor rooted in history's systems of oppression.

For Black men to heal from a masculinity that is traumatized and hypersexualized by the language of whiteness and that too often leads to pouring their untreated trauma over the bodies and beings of Black women. Intimate revolution means unlearning that Black women are Black men's emotional currency—having their value treated as a commodity—and replacing it with a path, process, and practice of making peace within their Black male bodies, and the complexity within themselves.

Resistance negotiation: for white women and men to do the emotional labor of staying to work through the discomfort—your insides that squirm, protest, deny, and defend as you are challenged, confronted, and called out about issues of race and racism. Resistance negotiation requires you to navigate through feeling personally maligned; it is how you stay, fight, and work through "white fragility," the term coined by Robin DiAngelo.

Revolutionary Black grace: for Black people globally to unlearn the narrative that makes American blackness criminal and African blackness wretched. It's unlearning a single-story narrative exported by the language of whiteness rooted in systems of oppression that sustain segregated Blackness and feed emotional labor that upholds unhealed, untreated trauma among global Black people. It is learning to love one another more justly as global Black people, and to engage one another with more compassion, tenderness, discernment, and empathy.

This is our work: to unlearn the language of whiteness and replace each of its pillars with an Emotional Justice love language. That means we must

- Unlearn emotional patriarchy and replace it with intimate reckoning.
- Unlearn racialized emotionality and replace it with resistance negotiation.
- Unlearn emotional currency and replace it with intimate revolution.
- Unlearn emotional economy and replace it with revolutionary Black grace.

Unlearning each pillar and replacing it with an Emotional Justice love language is our process, path, and practice for racial healing, dismantling systemic inequity, and building a truly brave new world that centers our full humanity, one that works for all peoples—Black, Brown, and Indigenous women and men, and white women and men.

The Emotional Justice Template

For each of us to do this emotional labor, there is the Emotional Justice template. While our work as Black, Brown, Indigenous, and white people is not the same, there are three steps we each must take to do that work:

- Work through our **feelings**
- Reimagine our **focus**
- Build the **future**

Work through our feelings. The feelings of flee, deny, disregard, blame, shame, punish, defend, grief, sadness, hurt, and leaning on historical behaviors will all come up. Leaning on historical behaviors means engaging in old racial disparity dynamics of Black emotional labor in service of whiteness. Become aware of these feelings; feel them—all of them. That's how we begin unlearning the language of whiteness. That awareness is a beginning. It is the act of becoming embodied.

For white women, that means no more "white tears"—the weaponizing of emotions to avoid doing your emotional labor when it comes to issues of race and racism.

For Black, Brown, and Indigenous women, that means not taking on the emotional labor of soothing, comforting, and reassuring whiteness. These feelings are part of an emotionally racial DNA—that is how a history of oppressive systems shapes the emotional responses and engagement of Black, Brown, and Indigenous people—and particularly women.

Reimagine our focus. Answer this question: How do I speak the language of whiteness? Answer it for yourself first and then within your community, your places of work and learning.

Build the future. For white people, this step entails decentering—focusing outside yourself and instead centering the experience of Black, Brown, and Indigenous people. Building this future means severing your emotional connection to whiteness that puts white people at the center. This severing is a continuous action, not a one and done. It is in this focus that you choose a different path, and start actively speaking an

Emotional Justice love language. This focus is transformative; it is the future.

For Black, Brown, and Indigenous people—and particularly women—building the future means actively centering yourself and ending the historical practice of soothing, comforting, and reassuring whiteness. By actively centering yourself, you start speaking an Emotional Justice love language. This is building your future doing your particular emotional labor.

This decentering for white people and centering for Black, Brown, and Indigenous peoples—and particularly women—is how we build a future with a racial healing practice. It is how we gain and practice Emotional Justice.

This Emotional Justice template requires that you stay, emotionally. What I mean by that is that you stay and feel all the feelings that emerge—resentment, denial, guilt, frustration, desire to flee, shame, sadness, grief, anger, hurt. It means you do not run from the feelings or project them onto someone else or punish someone because of how this emotional labor makes you feel. This is what it means to do your own emotional labor. It is what is necessary to then focus on answering the question, How do I speak the language of whiteness? And that focus leads you to create a future of developing and sustaining a racial healing practice, and speaking an Emotional Justice love language.

Examples of Change

We at The Armah Institute of Emotional Justice have seen how Emotional Justice training transforms worlds through these three steps. In the wake of the George Floyd murder and a national reckoning that ignited a focus on diversity, change, race, and healing, we led an Emotional Justice training at a department in an Ivy League university. The training is called Emotional Justice Truth and Accountability Sessions. This is a three-day workshop followed by a six-month facilitation to work with department heads to effect sustainable change.

We separated students and their department faculty, managers, and leadership. We held a full interactive and creative session where we asked Black and Brown students to describe the department's organizational culture. We were engaging a thirty-year span of past and present students. Whether they were alumni or current students, their narratives were disturbingly similar. Their answers revealed a narrative of elitism, an unwillingness to wrestle with or resolve issues of race when they arose, a disregard for their well-being, exclusionary and discriminatory practice, a world that was lily white.

The group included a Black student excited to participate in a department production, going for a wardrobe fitting that required a white coat. The costume department hadn't found anything for him, and told him he could wear a coat from a previous production. He put it on, and discovered it had KKK on it. KKK for Ku Klux Klan, the white supremacist group that terrorized Black people, burned crosses on lawns, and is part of a dark, dark period of American history. He was shocked by the costume department's nonchalant attitude toward him wearing that for rehearsal after rehearsal and then performance after performance without any care or thought of what that might mean for him. Wardrobe is a crucial part of a character in theater. The department's disregard for what that student needed, lack of care about his well-being and his performance, and lack of action when he raised how problematic this wardrobe was—all were symptomatic of his student experience in the department.

Other students shared that they had stopped going to auditions because of an ongoing inability to land roles that enabled them to practice their craft, and the department's use of a canon of material that was almost exclusively white. Another called out the way department productions were considered mainstage and desirable, but the single diverse theater body was in a basement and treated as if there was, in their words, "theatrical apartheid."

We asked the predominantly white faculty, managers, and department heads the same question about their experience of the organizational culture. They used words such as *inclusive, affirming, diverse, belonging,* and *engaging.*

We then presented our findings from our engagement with the students and alumni to the white faculty, managers, and department heads, using art and theater. With Emotional Justice training, we privilege narrative and use art and theater. Our training team includes artists. That's because while numbers offer information, narrative provides connection. Emotional Justice is about making connections you have not made before, both within you and to experiences outside yourself.

After presenting a dramatized written monologue encapsulating the students' findings, we asked for their feedback about what they heard. They shared their shock, and they spoke about the harm the department is doing to Black and Brown students, and their realization that they had not been centering Black and Brown students. After they shared their feedback, we invited them to describe that organizational culture, now centering their Black and Brown students. They no longer used words like *belonging* and *inclusive*; words such as *harming, discriminatory,* and *exclusionary* now appeared.

It does matter that we say the university policy celebrates diversity, affirms inclusivity, and firmly rejects discrimination. But we must remember that policy alone doesn't help us measure organizational culture. That's because policy is about your intention, whereas culture reveals your practice and your values. Culture is about outcome. And it is in culture that the hidden values of worth and who is centered reveal themselves. Whiteness always centers itself and measures success from its experience.

For white people, focusing on an experience outside yourself is an Emotional Justice practice of decentering. For this department, making that connection set a path to change the department's future, as well as that of both the students and those who teach and lead their department.

The department faculty and leadership described what the Emotional Justice training did for the department. One said, "Emotional Justice is decentering ourselves in order to move on from the painful structures that exist due to white supremacy." One department leader said, "Emotional Justice is coming to terms with what we are, not what we think we are, and it creates a path to inclusion." Another said, "Emotional Justice is repairing the damage of anti-Blackness and white supremacy."

Another example of Emotional Justice training takes place with Black, Brown, and Indigenous women leaders and managers to reimagine a relationship to labor and to center rest and replenishment. It is a three-part interactive, creative webinar training session called The Love Languages of Emotional Justice.

This means inviting women to explore their relationship to labor and rest rooted in family, history, and systems of oppression. The idea of institutionalizing their wellness and their rest, and centering it within a labor landscape, is difficult for many to grasp, so there is resistance.

In this training, we explore how the language of whiteness shapes Black, Brown, and Indigenous women's relationship to labor, how history made that relationship a life-and-death scenario, and how the legacy of the untreated trauma of that history has contemporary consequences. What we call *grind* is the modern manifestation of the historical relationships among labor, value, race, and gender.

During one training, we asked this group of women, "Where did you learn about grind? How does it show up in your world?" There was an outpouring, upset, sadness, and tears as women leaders spoke about lessons from mothers and grandfathers, about immigrant communities ingraining grind as the single route to success, how they as women leaders and managers perpetuated those lessons taught by their families, and how exhausted and debilitated the women felt. In this training, we treat trauma as an equity issue, and introduce what we call the Emotional Justice Equity Package, where wellness, rest, and replenishment are identified, budgeted, and monetized for the life cycle of a project as an act of unlearning whiteness, centering themselves, and catering to an institutionalizing of wellness.

One participant summed up what Emotional Justice did and what it meant for her, her organization, and community. She said, "I believe Emotional Justice is a way to begin to repair all the damage that oppressive systems have caused in our communities. It is a way of recognizing our humanity beyond what we produce."

As we see, our work is not the same. But we all have our emotional work to do. This is our practice, our path, and our process—engage it every time, and we strengthen our Emotional

Justice muscles. We develop a practice of racial healing. It guides us to be better, to move in justice with one another in unprecedented ways.

We have to know what we are changing, and we have to know what we are changing it into. Emotional Justice means calculating the cost, recognizing the toll, and unlearning the story of the language of whiteness by challenging and changing when, how, and for whom we use our voice, our emotional labor, and our power. By doing our particular emotional work, we can love one another more justly because of a sustainable practice of Emotional Justice.

What Is an Emotional Justice Love Language?

Love. That four-letter word that centers on feeling good, affirmed, uplifted, desired. Our understanding of a love language is based on Dr. Gary Chapman's *The 5 Love Languages*, a global best seller that taught people five ways we speak the language of love in our intimate relationships, and how learning those languages nurtures and sustains our intimate relationships. Understanding love languages make our relationships better. An Emotional Justice love language for racial healing makes our racial healing journey possible—and transforms it into an ultimately sustainable practice.

When it comes to race, we have too often wanted a weird, unrealistic, and unattainable "Let's all just love each other" love—one that is all-encompassing, one that blurs color, disappears conflict, and centers on how much good we all want to do and how at heart we are all the same, just good people. I get that. But an Emotional Justice love language is not that.

To be clear, you will feel absolutely wonderful, empowered, engaged, and affirmed—but perhaps not at first. The Emotional Justice love languages are about a journey into places that are rife with discomfort, where you feel challenged and where you might not want to be. It is in that precise place that the love begins. And it is in this place that you are called to stay.

An Emotional Justice love language will—and should—stretch our emotional muscles in directions that are unfamiliar. In other words, there are unrecognized places we all must go that, as part of this Emotional Justice love language, change our bodies in ways that surprise, delight, threaten, and infuriate.

It is what you then do with those feelings that makes this an Emotional Justice love language. Deep listening is part of an Emotional Justice language of comprehension, of understanding and being understood. Right now, when it comes to race, too many of us listen as a defense mechanism against a "You're being racist" accusation. We double down, fling out phrases about no regrets, reliance on good intentions, accountability-free accountability, and unrelenting deflection from actually holding, having, and staying in hard conversations on racism, white supremacy, and racial healing.

With an Emotional Justice love language, accountability no longer feels like oppression, consequence is the inevitable cost of racial harm, intention is not a defense that excuses consequence for racial harm, and advocacy is as integral a part of an organization's equity and antiracist practice as silence had been before our worlds changed unimaginably in 2020.

An Emotional Justice love language means speaking out and speaking up without requiring applause or affirmation, and wrestling with your own fear of repercussions or punishment.

Speaking out and speaking up are crucial steps in doing dismantling work, which leads to developing a racial healing practice. To walk this road less traveled, we need compassion, equity, and empathy. All of those things are hard within a climate torn apart by an unrelenting violence, bolstered by a deeply divisive politics, and protected by the kind of policy that rewards behavior that traumatizes and devastates millions.

Here's the thing—someone else can't speak an Emotional Justice love language for you. Right now, some of us claim victims' rights at the merest hint of racial impropriety, slinging emotional arrows left and right in our valiant bid to evade doing this work. Some speak the language of avoidance fluently. In other words, the let's-just-talk-about-something-else-anything-else-ology. Or we think this work should be done according to that clock called only-so-much-discomfort-then-I'm-out. We may speak the language of "cancel culture," that ferocious means of communicating where we play prosecutor, judge, jury, and executioner, elevating fear and desecrating the will for courageous conversations in troubled racial territory—such a necessity in racial healing work—but are reduced to sparring, to jabs in a social media ring where gloves are off and the goal is to draw blood.

For too long, too many of us have believed that this work can and should be done by one side, by one people, by changing behaviors, by reimagining transformation as tweaking, then standing back with a self-congratulatory *Ta-da!* at our barely there efforts. Tweaking. That shit doesn't work. It never has. It is a ruse; it is reckoning-avoidance. And for too long, too many have expected to be incentivized to do this emotional work. An Emotional Justice love language is one you learn rooted in your belief in and your commitment to a fairer world, a more humane one.

Here's the beauty: a new language is a gift enabling us to communicate beyond our worlds and move into terrain that may be terrifying, but now with tools and resources. Here's the challenge: How willing are we to learn a language that helps us do the emotional work to create the world we believe in philosophically or ideologically, one where Black lives matter? How willing are we to make that language real in our worlds—of work, of education, of policy, of justice? Here's the breakthrough: we can all learn a new language.

A Legacy of Untreated Trauma

Untreated trauma is a thread that runs through this emotional connection to and relationship with whiteness, race, and power from a legacy of oppressive systems. Let's define trauma. It is a deeply distressing or disturbing experience. It is damage, a wound, hurt that has lasting consequences beyond one body but also intergenerationally, handed down, manifesting again and again.

For millions of people, George Floyd's killing was their closest engagement with racial trauma—being witness through the power of social media and the courage of a Black teenage girl who captured every heartbreaking second. For millions, this killing was a single act that led to an awakening about racial terror and law enforcement in America. For millions of Black people globally, it was not a single act but the cumulative effect of a policing system unpunished and unaccountable, whose violence robs families of loved ones with deadly regularity.

For millions of white people, George Floyd's murder was transformative, it was a discovery; for millions of Black people, it was traumatizing and triggering—igniting both ancestral memory of white authority murdering Black people and feelings of helplessness, rage, and grief. It was untreated trauma.

For Black people globally, Floyd's murder was a deep wound that reaches beyond America's shores and into the UK, South Africa, across Europe—where families have fought the state and its police systems that have killed outside of video, minus criminal justice consequence, but have been no less devastating.

In setting off on your journey to learn an Emotional Justice love language, you will encounter this untreated trauma that manifests in ways that may confuse, frustrate, or transform you. The way to speak the love language and use it as a tool is to recognize that such encounters are part of what occurs when you are doing Emotional Justice labor. You may feel confused, but it is here where you should feel encouraged. This is part of racial healing with the Emotional Justice roadmap.

How I Built the
Emotional Justice Roadmap

I developed this roadmap over fifteen years within a global community of activists, activist leaders, scholars, artists, and journalists in four cities in four countries across three continents. I built it with two components:

- Research

- Engagement

The research was through assignments in the US, the UK, and Africa that opened my eyes to the unnamed and unacknowledged power of the emotional when it came to race, power, politics, and whiteness. The engagement came with living and working in the US for nearly eight years and expanding that research through curated conversations exploring a legacy of untreated trauma that shapes how we see ourselves and each other as Black and white people.

Unlearning the language of whiteness requires internal and external work for us all. In other words, there is the personal reckoning that requires our own behavior and actions to be challenged and changed, and there is work to be done structurally, within and by all the sectors and systems we are all part of. That work needs to expand and continue in order for those systems to change. Let's be clear: it is the interconnection of the internal and the external that is crucial, that is a foundational part of an Emotional Justice love language. Personal change alone ain't it. That change must expand to be applied within the systems and sectors of labor, learning, leisure, beauty, entertainment, governance—all of them. We have all been shaped by the dual history of dangerous and deadly delusions: white superiority and Black inferiority. We pay a price for both.

I went on my own journey to devise, develop, and design the Emotional Justice roadmap. I'll share what that looked like. Let's hit the road.

• 2 •

The Unfinished Journey of Racial Healing

I t is 1997. I travel to Ghana, Philadelphia, and South Africa. These three assignments form the foundation and lead to the naming of Emotional Justice. In making my journey, I discover that racial healing has its own journey. I learn what that journey looks like and, crucially, what it lacks. I learn that the journey is unfinished. In fact, a racial healing journey doesn't have an arrival destination; I learn that it must be a practice, developed, sustained, and engaged by us and by generations that come after us.

Ghana, 1997

I am here to cover forty years of independence from British colonial rule. My dad was an activist in pre-Independence Ghana, a fierce pan-Africanist with equally fierce sideburns who would go on and become a diplomat and a minister serving in the government of Ghana's first president, Kwame Nkrumah.

During this assignment, my mother breaks her twenty-plus-year silence about Ghana's first military coup in February

1966. She reveals that she faced the tanks, the soldiers, and their violence.

My mother is a woman of tribe and faith—proudly Christian and Ashanti. The 1966 coup incarcerated my dad, turned us out of our home and our nation. Three in the morning my mother tells me. That's when the tanks roll up to our front door, soldiers in battle fatigues and black boots stomping, breaking down our door, and ransacking our home. They smash all the windows, break cupboards, turn out drawers. They put a gun to her head. They terrify and terrorize us. One night is followed by two years under house arrest. Soldiers' battle fatigues become part of our home.

I have no memory of the night or the following two years. For over twenty years I am haunted by night terrors where I am dragged awake at 3 a.m. hearing black boots stomping all around my head. When my mother broke her silence, it was a discovery for me.

The discovery was about naming what is hidden, and the power of what is hidden to shape you in ways that you cannot understand until and unless what is hidden is both named and put into context. It is in this naming and contextualizing that I begin to think about who I am as an emotional human being, outside of profession and education. I am an educated, professional young woman who is struggling and does not understand why. I learn you cannot PhD your way out of trauma.

I speak with others. Kwame Nkrumah's eldest son shares his story and memory. Later, when I return to London I speak with Paul Boateng, the UK's first Black cabinet minister, and he shares his memory. Their memories are versions of my own, of boots, of homes turned battleground, of soldiers and guns, of home turned horror.

From each of these stories, I explore more about the world of the emotional and its power. I learn how the emotional—

your relationship to yourself—is shaped, and how that shaping is not necessarily changed or healed by just intellectual focus or educational achievement.

I learn that the emotional has a power unconnected to the intellectual, the professional, and the educational. This discovery is a signpost pointing to the power of naming, of finding language to identify what has been hidden. It marks the beginning of a journey to recognize the power of the emotional. It's step 1 in the research process.

Philadelphia, 1997

I am here to cover the October 1997 Million Woman March. I meet Winnie Mandela, the march's keynote speaker—a celebrated and, for some, controversial choice.

I had never been to Philadelphia—or the US at that point. I stay with a nice white liberal woman who has kindly opened up her home to Black women traveling to Philadelphia for the march. Her home is large, and other nice white liberal folks rent rooms from her. She, and they, are deeply upset by the choice of Winnie Mandela as the keynote speaker.

There are multiple conversations about their concern. I am struck by how angry they are, and I am especially struck by how much they think their anger should be considered—wrong word, actually; they feel that it should be centered—by Black women at an event that is about Black women. This is where I really notice how whiteness centers itself and expects the emotions of white people to be not simply acknowledged but centered and acted on, overriding how those emotions impact a Black woman and something that matters to that Black woman.

The question my host consistently asks me is, What are you doing here? At first I am puzzled by the question. She had opened up her home for a Black woman. And ain't I a Black woman? She asks the question again and again. Eventually I ask if there was an issue. Immediately defensive, she shushes me. I am more surprised than annoyed. I end up meeting her dad, who, it turns out, is a real-life missionary who worked in Ghana. He asks me the same question: What are you doing here? He elaborates. He was told that my family is from Ghana, from Africa, and I was born and live in Britain. To him, I don't look like I need help. *Weird*, I thought. I explain—as I had done many, many times to his daughter—that I am a journalist, covering the march, and need accommodation, that I am Black British, and that yes, my family is from Ghana. Father and daughter exchange looks. *Weird*, I thought. Discomfort hangs in the air. It lingers. So weird. I learn that to this father and daughter I don't look like a "needy" Black woman. I don't look wretched, and I don't seem poor. Their attitude is ludicrous to me. And it leads me to a realization. Their relationship to Blackness—particularly one that derived from Africa—is about a certain wretchedness, an inability, a body needing saving. I don't fit the narrative.

This experience helps me explore the emotional power of the language of whiteness as a narrative of how the world is, our place in it as white and Black people, and how that language shapes how we may see each other.

I am at Philadelphia's Eakins Oval, both a historical site of slave auctions and the Million Woman March stage. It is where Winnie Mandela delivers her keynote to thousands and thousands of women stretched from Benjamin Franklin Parkway right down to Penn's Landing and spilling over to City Hall.

I share with Winnie Mandela a story Pa shared with me. He welcomed to Ghana Umkontho we Sizwe, the armed wing of the African National Congress. They came to train, fight, and take up armed struggle as resistance to apartheid's white supremacist terror that was destroying Black people.

I tell Mrs. Mandela about Ma, her broken silence and the night the tanks came. I tell her I am headed to her home nation of South Africa to engage the global narrative and conversation on forgiveness, as part of an assignment on the globally renowned Truth and Reconciliation Commission.

Mama Winnie—as she is affectionately called in South Africa and by global Black folk—reminds me that as I travel in South Africa, I need to center my mother's broken silence and to think more deeply about what she endured. She reminds me to connect Ma's silence as a Black woman in thinking through and exploring forgiveness by Black people of white racist violence.

That begins a journey to center Black women in understanding how a nation's narrative is shaped, whom it centers, and whom it excludes, and how that exclusion shapes the story of who they are as a people.

This assignment—meeting and speaking with Winnie, the exchanges with the nice white liberal woman and her dad—was a consciousness-raising moment. I hadn't thought deeply about gender and whiteness in a conscious way. I hadn't really thought critically about gender, Blackness, and healing until then either. I was beginning to.

South Africa, 1997

I report on the Truth and Reconciliation Commission (TRC), the body set up following South Africa's first democratic elections in 1994. The commission's focus: tell the full truth about the atrocities you committed during apartheid, and in return, you get amnesty. I meet and interview Archbishop Desmond Tutu (now deceased), the commission's architect and an anti-apartheid warrior; and Ntsiki Biko, the widow of Steve Biko, a beloved figure known as South Africa's Black Father of Consciousness. It is November 1997.

Covering the TRC, I, like the global media, watch this wrenching truth-telling process of an outpouring of Black trauma against white legislated violence. It is here that I explore and develop the language of whiteness and name two of its pillars, emotional patriarchy and racialized emotionality. These first two pillars become integral parts of unlearning this language of whiteness. Naming these two pillars occurs after two encounters: the first is a pivotal interview with Desmond Tutu; the second is after listening to Ntsiki Biko, the widow of Steve Biko.

I am ushered into Archbishop Tutu's office in Cape Town. He prays before our interview. I ask him about this process of forgiveness between white and Black people.

"South Africa will be a Mecca for whites, just like Kenya!" declares Tutu. I ask him why there's so much focus on how white people feel. His answer is evasive. I ask again. And again. I ask why there is so much focus on how white people feel in a nation healing from so much horror and harm perpetrated against Black bodies by a system that enshrined the false superiority of whiteness. He gets uncomfortable and then angry.

He tells me that when it comes to repair, Black South Africans shouldn't ask for too much. I ask him what "too much" means, given the extent, weight, and depth of pain caused to Black South Africans and their families. He goes on to explain that if someone needs particular assistance—say, a wheelchair—because of apartheid violence, then the person could get that. The TRC would find someone to help them with that. I am struck by how limited the language of repair is, but also how individual it is. Even though the TRC body is about forgiving an entire people, the repair seems to be about forgetting that an entire people had been subject to apartheid.

I continue to ask about Black people's needs, and their healing. Tutu then says, "The whites are beginning to take this offer of forgiveness for granted." I am especially struck by this. The interview comes to an end—honestly, it was cut short by Archbishop Tutu's team. I leave with a sharpened focus on this centralizing and soothing of whiteness and a neglect of Blackness.

Archbishop Tutu mentioned Kenya. A mecca for whites just like Kenya, he said. Kenya fought the British for its independence. During colonial rule in Kenya, the British committed violent atrocities. They tortured, raped, and murdered. They imprisoned 1.6 million Kikuyu—an entire population—in a violent attempt to suppress the growing battle for independence. Jomo Kenyatta was Kenya's first post-Independence president. After Kenya gained its independence, in 1964, Kenyatta would tell the British, let's forgive and forget. There are archival images, articles, and interviews of him reassuring white Britons that Kenya forgives them, and that this land continues to be their home.

I have familial connection in Kenya too. My dad had been an advisor to Jomo Kenyatta. He too was an advocate of reconciliation. In our home in Ghana, there are black-and-white images of my dad with Kenyatta. Years later, I travel to Kenya on an assignment that deepens my understanding of a history of racial healing that firmly centers whiteness.

Forgive and Forget:
Race and the Language of Whiteness

Nelson Mandela would echo Jomo Kenyatta's words of forgiveness. "Let bygones be bygones. Let what has happened pass as something unfortunate which we must forget," he said, speaking of South Africa's future in one of several interviews following his release from twenty-seven years in prison.

What was Mandela asking South Africa to forget, to forgive? The laws enshrining false notions of white superiority and Black inferiority. That included laws such as the Urban Areas Act of 1923, which created what became exclusive African slums. The 1926 Color Bar Act, which banned Africans from practicing skilled trades and forced a poverty that Black South Africans continue to struggle with today. The 1936 Representation of Natives Act, which removed Black voters from the common voters' roll in Cape Town, thereby denouncing their citizenhood.

What Mandela was asking to let pass was the water cannons, the truncheons, the torture, and the killing and terrorizing of children, robbing them of their innocence, their childhood, making violence their normal. There was the killing and raping of women, the murder of men's souls, the murder of men's bodies. There was the emasculation of Black men, the humiliation of Black women, the wholesale thievery of land. There was racializing and dehumanizing Black bodies and then targeting them with ongoing violence.

Forgiveness, then, took on a color, a context, a direction, and a meaning. Apartheid was terrorism and white supremacy. Forgiveness was Black emotional labor, and it was absolution for whiteness. It was a one-and-done healing scenario. It did not account for legacy, and didn't center those who had been harmed and what was necessary for their healing. That meant white people did no emotional work, but received amnesty and forgiveness.

It is in my realization of this context of forgiveness that I coin the term *racialized emotionality*—describing a world where we racialize emotions, where we insert color, context, and consequence to emotions—and where doing so changes how we see those bodies in whom the emotions have been racialized.

Years later, I connect this history of racial healing, of emotional labor by Black folk in service of white supremacist violence, to the US and the UK.

Creating a Racial Healing Roadmap

South Africa's racial healing model, one that is emulated and lauded by countries all over the world, was not constructed centering—or really even fully acknowledging—Black and Brown people and the breadth and depth of the harm, the toll, and the legacy of that harm on them and their communities. Because of that, this was not a roadmap for racial healing. Instead, it was a model that privileges one group and exacts emotional labor from another. It was political, it was structural, and it was inequitable. It was an unfinished journey.

No national or global conversation about forgiveness centered Black people forgiving themselves and one another for what they had endured, for what they became, for how this shaped how they loved, for the self-hate that survival may have triggered, and for the toll that eternally fighting took on their sense of self.

One of the most powerful examples is in the treatment of Winnie Mandela. South African writer Sisonke Msimang wrote, "This was a nation with a narrative of forgiveness, but it wouldn't forgive Winnie Mandela." There was public humiliation and global castigation of a Black woman, while De

Klerk, a white man who never stood on a global platform professing the horrors perpetrated by South African governments on its Black citizens, received a Nobel Peace Prize.

In saying let bygones be bygones, what Nelson Mandela and the TRC did was ask Black people, brutalized and beaten, to privilege the fears, insecurities, and feelings of white folk over their own sacrifice, story, and struggles and those of their families. And the world applauded, in awe of this capacity for forgiveness, and turned Mandela into an icon of forgiveness.

This model of racial healing—both in South Africa and in Kenya—is an emotional apartheid. It separates white and Black people. It is a model that entrenches inequity by centering whiteness and reinforcing emotional labor as the work of Black folk, and white folks as the recipients of that emotional labor. It timelines and deadlines the trauma for those harmed, treating the emotional as if it were an economy, to be moved and manipulated.

It is this inequity that strengthens already existing labor disparities around race. From physical labor to emotional labor by Black people in service of whiteness, this was emotional injustice. And in this time, we cannot take that approach if we are to achieve a racial healing that serves a full humanity.

Ntsiki Biko and a Journey of Deeper Understanding

A pivotal exchange with Ntsiki Biko creates the term *Emotional Justice* and, for me, solidifies the need, the work, and the roadmap. She stood before the world's predominantly white media and invited them to better understand what happened to her husband, Steve Biko. She told them that, for her, there was no question of forgiveness.

Ten former members of the security branch of the South Africa police sought amnesty for Steve Biko's death. They said that Steve Biko, in the presence of the white policemen, had "gone berserk" during a "scuffle," which led to his death.

Addressing the Truth and Reconciliation hearing, one said: "Your honor, we have said that during the scuffle, he bumped his head against the wall."

"Scuffle" and "bumped"? The so-called scuffle was a twenty-two-hour interrogation involving ten officers. Biko was shackled, and his legs were put in leg irons. The "bump" resulted in a battered and bruised body, left naked, then transported to Pretoria, rather than given medical treatment. It was a Black body they then put in a cell naked, and left to die.

The TRC's process required the full truth to be told. Those who took the stand regarding Steve Biko's death didn't do that. They prettied up brutality, justified terror, minimalized violence, and expected forgiveness.

Ntsiki Biko said, "There is a lot of talk about reconciliation. What I want is for the proper course of justice to be done." Mrs. Biko and other families sued the government, rejecting the TRC's process and demanding justice for their loved ones.

It is listening to Mrs. Biko, her call for a justice even when connected to a process that was deeply emotional, that I begin to think in a more structural way about the emotional and Blackness as integral parts of a justice project.

Lessons from Ntsiki Biko, Desmond Tutu, and the TRC

I begin to parse and rearrange the pieces of this narrative about pain, power, race, whiteness, emotional labor, and racial healing. I am struck by the focus on how white people feel, by the care and thought given to those feelings, and by how those feelings are the center of a process that addressed forgiveness—by how the pain and loss were racialized and politicized. The process was not individual—it was structural and one connected to the political, but it was unjust and inhumane.

I begin connecting the emotional to the notion of justice when it comes to race through listening to Ntsiki Biko, to Winnie, and to the women of South Africa, and through my interviews with Desmond Tutu and other ANC leaders. I don't judge their focus; I simply recognize that this is unfinished work. Effective racial healing—through which Black and white people come to fuller humanity—cannot be achieved by centering the needs, the fears, and the feelings of those who have caused the harm. Because when we do that, we are using the emotional as an instrument to entrench what is unjust. That teaches the perpetrator entitlement, and it teaches those harmed to sideline themselves.

I see how this model manifests all the way up to the world of DEI (diversity, equity, and inclusion). It is a model that centers those who hold power and have abused it. It centers their feelings and discomfort. It calls for minimal labor by those who perpetuate harm, and applauds, affirms, and appreciates them for doing the bare minimum—and then calls that change.

I see how this model manifests during the trial of Dylan Roof, the white American supremacist mass murderer who killed nine African Americans in church. He stood in the dock as the loved ones of those killed offered an outpouring of forgiveness, emotion, tears, and trauma toward this white supremacist murderer.

Let me be clear. I do not condemn individual acts of forgiveness by those who believe in that. This is about a global racial healing model, the lessons passed down by that model, and how those lessons shape what we do today—but, more important, what we do not do. This is about understanding that there has been no equal division of emotional labor; there has barely been a requirement that white people do any emotional labor on behalf of dismantling inequity. And it is for this reason that we need Emotional Justice and its roadmap for racial healing.

Emotional Justice Is Born

It is because of my journey with these assignments—engaging with leaders, listening to Black South African women challenging authority, and watching an adoring global media lap up the South African model—that the term *Emotional Justice* is fully born. It is because of my journey that I explore how systems are upheld and that I more fully understand that systems work through people, are maintained by people, and therefore must be dismantled by people. The individual connects to the institutional. Context, nuance, and detail matter. The emotional work is the crucial—but neglected—part of the political, intellectual, and organizing work to dismantle white supremacy.

This historical but now outdated racial healing model lauded in South Africa—one of white harm and Black forgiveness, Black outpouring of pain and trauma, white supremacy and Black emotional labor—promoted injustice. There was no reckoning, wrestling, or negotiating for whiteness—and therefore no dismantling of systemic inequity, no racial healing practice that addressed a full humanity. The emotional required justice too.

Emotional Justice is ignited by my mother's broken silence, expanded by Winnie Mandela's words of guidance, cemented by Ntsiki Biko's act of resistance. It is also shaped by the men of the movement: my dad, Nelson Mandela, and Archbishop Tutu, who taught me that the political was upheld and entrenched by the emotional. Their work was crucial in shaping the course of independence for African nations and must always be celebrated and honored. There is simultaneously undone, unrecognized, unnamed work—that work needs a new model. Reconciliation is not, and cannot be, the path for racial healing for our future and our humanity. Emotional Justice is.

Emotional Justice is about all of us having emotional work to do, but as I stated earlier in this book, that work is not the same, the harm is not the same, the toll is not the same. South Africa's lesson for me—and Kenya's before it—was that the old model of racial healing began by centering whiteness. Such a beginning could bring no healing to a humanity harmed by this whiteness—not for white or Black people. Understanding mattered, and so the roadmap for racial healing was named.

The Engagement

New York, 2009-2014

I live and work in New York for seven years. I absorb the lessons from South Africa and Kenya about the damage of centering whiteness. I build on those lessons and explore how they connect in the US and with US history. Here, I expand what I experienced in London, learned in Ghana, developed in Philadelphia, and manifested in South Africa.

In New York, I specifically center Blackness. I lead annual public intimate discussion and conversation series across multiple platforms. One example is the Brecht Forum in Manhattan. It is the first home to and sacred space for #EJconvos, a five-year annual series of discussions with activists, scholars, artists, journalists, and public intellectuals, engaging with community who come to listen, share, and challenge. Our first seasons grapple with trauma, the power of emotions and the emotional to shape, stifle, and stall movements no matter how sound and strong their politics. I explore the critical—but misunderstood and ignored—role of the emotional in what is too often defined as purely ideological, philosophical, or intellectual.

Scholar Mark Anthony Neal; award-winning filmmaker Byron Hurt; scholar, writer, and television commentator Marc Lamont Hill; and scholar and writer Dumi L'Heureux Lewis make up the very first New York #EJconvos panel. We explore Black male privilege within our own communities, whom and how it hurts, and how we might heal.

#EJconvos navigates the personal, familial, and political trauma; Blackness; movements; power and change. In other words, it explores and identifies our emotional work as Black people when it comes to racial healing. This annual series of discussions includes award-winning writer Akiba Solomon; critically acclaimed writer and scholar Dr. Joan Morgan; scholar and *New York Times* best-selling author Dr. Brittney Cooper; award-winning poet, writer, and activist Staceyann Chin; educator and child-rights activist Dr. Stacey Patton; national radio host Karen Hunter; writer and activist Darnell Moore; scholar Rich Blint; and organizer and leader Wade Davis II, among many others.

I explore how Emotional Justice can change, challenge, and shape the way that white women progressives do their work; and in conversation with activist, writer, and educator Jennifer JLove Calderon; *New York Times* best-selling author and journalist Laura Flanders; journalist and educator Jennifer Pozner; and racial justice educator Marjery Freeman, we explore what that work is and why it is so crucial. Jennifer JLove Calderon goes on to engage Emotional Justice in her work regarding liberation and challenging white people. She would say of Emotional Justice, "As a white woman focused and committed to working with white people to tackle our biases and focus on an antiracism practice, Emotional Justice is a powerful, purpose-filled framework that I engage with— and can call on my community to engage. I worked with Esther and her framework for all of my work."

What starts and is explored and developed in South Africa, Kenya, and London expands to the US. This expansion identifies Emotional Justice as a global model and roadmap for racial healing.

On the Stage

From holding annual in-person series, I move to a more creative space to enable me to more deeply think through themes of Blackness, identity, emotionality, and power. The theater becomes the space to deepen the roadmap, expand its meaning, and further engage the community through new audiences. There are performances and panels in New York and Chicago, where I write four plays and have them produced and performed.

On the Mic

The airwaves are a home for me to explore racial healing that centers and explores Blackness. I am a radio host of *Wakeup Call*, the morning show of WBAI, the New York radio station of independent national broadcaster Pacifica. I conduct a series of one-on-one exchanges on the mic. With my guests, I explore how the emotional shows up to stifle and shape individual lives, and connect individual experience to institutional work—that of movements, organizations, and sectors. These interviews include the notable scholar and writer Cornel West; scholar and writer Michael Eric-Dyson; and writer and feminist Rebecca Walker, daughter of Alice Walker.

I then create *The Spin*, a podcast with online and on-air audiences; it airs on community radio stations across the US—in Arizona, Mississippi, North Carolina, New Jersey, Connecticut, and South Carolina. The podcast has a specifically gendered and racial focus. Learning lessons from South Africa, remembering how affected I am by my mother's broken silence—I use this podcast and space to explore the world through the lens of Black women from academia, activism, journalism, and entrepreneurship, bringing together women in the US with those in Africa.

Expanding Emotional Justice, Creating Global Connections

I connect the legacy of racist US laws undone by resistance and social justice movements to those of South Africa and Kenya. I see how nurtured intellect, ideology, and profession are no substitute for doing the emotional work. I name racial healing that centers global Black people, navigating a legacy of untreated trauma due to the language of whiteness, language that has shaped a relationship to Blackness. I recognize how deeply ingrained the language of whiteness is in us all, even though it manifests in different ways. In South Africa and Kenya, I noted a deference to whiteness that shaped power, and an internalizing of historical trauma by the Black majority that would show up within community, how we treated and saw one another as global Black people.

The racial trauma from systems of oppression is not healed by legislation, ideology, or movements alone, although they hold a crucial place in transforming landscapes—and indeed landscapes are transformed by each of them. The emotional transforms us and how we see ourselves, and that needs healing in order for us to divest from a cycle of progress and regress.

2014-2019

I leave New York and travel to Ghana. Here I expand Emotional Justice further, and begin work on specific issues of masculinity, gender, violence, and healing a global Blackness shaped by the legacy of colonialism. I return to the keyboard and publications, exploring Emotional Justice in the context of Africa through a weekly column in Ghana's prestigious newspaper *Business & Financial Times*, and a writing series in *WARSCAPES*, an online space that explores conflict and is led by professor and writer Dr. Bhakti Shringarpure. I contribute Emotional Justice essays to the works of the critically acclaimed and award-winning writers Dr. Ibram X. Kendi and Dr. Keisha Blain.

2019-Present

I build a global institute, The Armah Institute of Emotional Justice. With a global team across Ghana, Chicago in the US, and London and Oxfordshire in the UK, we work to implement Emotional Justice as a tool to transform and heal within organizations and communities. It is for the global community of Black, Brown, Indigenous, and white humanity. We use storytelling as a strategy for structural change and develop our resources in three areas: projects, training, and thought leadership. Our work is to strategize, structuralize, and operationalize changing hearts and minds by developing resources and tools using the Emotional Justice roadmap.

So, from Ghana to London to Philadelphia to South Africa to New York, I make connections to the emotional work required to unlearn the language of whiteness as a crucial element for dismantling systemic inequity.

I Built This . . . in Global Community

This, then, is my journey of building the Emotional Justice roadmap for racial healing with family and global community in cities and countries and continents, through research and exchange; engaging storytelling, deep listening, journalism, theater, and history. Emotional Justice emerges from the ideas, the experiences, the history of horror and harm, of resistance and community, and lessons learned. It is the combination of all of these that forms the roadmap.

Emotional Justice ignites a global clarion call for finishing our journey with a roadmap for racial healing that takes heed of the models of South Africa and Kenya, recognizes the unacknowledged power of the emotional and the urgent need to connect it to justice, and expands to root it in a long line of justice movements to progress our world and dismantle what is inequitable. It is the roadmap to help finish this journey of racial healing for Black, Brown, Indigenous, and white people.

Chapters 1 and 2 explained how I built Emotional Justice through research and engagement. Now that I have shared how I built it, we're off to engage with it.

In the next four chapters, I introduce, define, and contextualize each of the four Emotional Justice love languages, the demographic they apply to, and what unlearning the language of whiteness looks like, and I end with the Emotional

Justice template to guide the action to be taken. Consider these next four chapters as your working tools, designed to be returned to again and again, to be engaged, explored, exchanged, and utilized in your worlds of labor and learning.

Each chapter includes the following elements:

- Definition and Action to Be Taken. This explains the love language and whom it applies to.
- Breakdown. This offers context for the love language and describes what unlearning the language of whiteness looks like in this context.
- An Exchange. This is a conversation with leaders and thinkers exploring what this work means to and for them and their sector.

At the end of each chapter, there is the three-step Emotional Justice template to help you work through the themes. As a reminder, they are

1. Work through your **feelings**
2. Reimagine your **focus**
3. Build the **future**

Let's now continue our journey together delving into each of the love languages of Emotional Justice. Let's keep going.

• 3 •

Intimate
Reckoning

Definition and Action to Be Taken

For white women and men to engage, challenge, and change their emotional relationship to power and race by doing the emotional labor of unlearning the language of whiteness. That means ending the practice of *emotional patriarchy*. This unlearning is both a process and a practice for white women and men that can make them game changers and change agents within communities of white people. It helps create a world where all people's humanity is centered.

Breakdown

Intimate reckoning is the specific emotional labor of white women and white men. It is an emotional labor they have not done before, and it is a particularly gendered labor. This work is about white men's emotional relationship to power and race and white women's role in sustaining that relationship, which profits and punishes them. White women are the designated worriers about the state of white masculinity. Through their own behaviors and engagement with race, they play a pivotal role in sustaining white men's emotional relationship to power and race. Dismantling the language of whiteness requires different work from different people. This work, white women's and white men's work, is about intimacy.

Intimacy as Institution

Intimacy is the place—precious, crucial, and powerful—where the whiteness narrative is nurtured. It is the single most supportive, unchallenged relationship when it comes to sustaining the language of whiteness in the bodies and breath of white men by white women. The whiteness narrative is part of how we develop a sense of ourselves and our place. Change it, and we change worlds. Challenge it, and we choose justice. Leave it as it is, and we are key change agents in protecting murderers of justice. Intimacy is where the language of whiteness is most fluent. Our emotional relationship to power manifests because of this fluency in whiteness via intimacy, and that is why it is crucial that this Emotional Justice love language is an "intimate reckoning."

There are two types of intimacy: private and public. Private intimacy is about relationships and community—family, church, extended family. Public intimacy is about the professional and the political: professional intimacy as in our places of work and education; political intimacy as in our places of governance, and our vote. It is through intimacy that emotional patriarchy flourishes and the language of whiteness is sustained. And it is here that substantive emotional labor takes place to uphold whiteness. That substantive emotional labor manifests in entrenched inequity.

Intimacy is an institution and system within Emotional Justice. It is built and maintained by an emotional ecosystem that protects and provides for the language of whiteness and white masculinity. White women protect the narrative and provide the dedicated, consistent, unwavering emotional labor to sustain it.

So it is through intimacy that unlearning the language of whiteness—ending emotional patriarchy—is pivotal, because it is through intimacy that the language of whiteness is most powerfully protected. Because of this specific power, an intimate reckoning is crucial for any real racial healing to occur and to be sustained. That's because intimacy is not a one and done. It is a way of being with each other; it is an ongoing relationship that emerges and evolves; it has strength because it has stakes; it is where our sense of self is affirmed, sustained, and upheld. These aspects of intimacy demand that the language of whiteness, which manifests as emotional patriarchy, must be replaced with intimate reckoning. It is in this space that emotional work is specifically required.

Whiteness: The Narrative

But first . . . white people will need to BREATHE. Because when white people hear the phrase *the language of whiteness* and about the need to unlearn it, they immediately get defensive, uncomfortable, and pissed. It feels like an attack. The defense mechanisms kick in, and the explaining, excusing, and negating go into full effect. That's because white people conflate "white people" with "the language of whiteness."

They are not the same thing.

The language of whiteness is a narrative. It's a narrative we are all taught, about how the world came to be, and our place in it as white, Black, Brown people—women, men, children. It is a story of who you are to whiteness, and what whiteness is to you.

Languages are made up of words and phrases; we learn how to pronounce them, how they go together in order for us to communicate. Did you learn French at school?

Teacher: Class, repeat after me: Bonjour.

Class: Bonjour.

Teacher: Good job! That means "Good day" in French.

The language of whiteness ain't French. It's not made up of words that we translate and that mean the same thing to any French-speaking person. No. It is spoken through how we see ourselves as global Black, Brown, Indigenous, and white people, and its meanings are fractured through the lens of how we see one another and how we are seen. The language of whiteness is about how we live and engage. It is the story of who we have been told we are, who we can and cannot be. It is a story that is a lethal, deadly fiction—treated as fact.

You can choose not to learn French. You can't choose not to learn the language of whiteness. The language of whiteness is not simply taught; it is enforced. It was birthed in sure, swift, brutal, and deadly historical systems: enslavement, colonialism, and apartheid. Each was violent. These systems were about separation and superiority; they produced narratives of struggle, salvation, survival, and surrender. They were about Black and white.

These systems have contemporary consequences that manifest in our world to this very day. They carry a lingering legacy of untreated trauma that manifests in each of us, in all of us. And we all live with and deal with that legacy and its manifestations.

Winners and Losers

This language of whiteness is about winning and winners, conquering and conquerors, saving and saviors. In *White Fragility*, white American author Robin DiAngelo writes about "navigating white people's internalized assumption of racial superiority"—that assumption is born of these historical systems. They nurtured an addiction to false notions of white superiority and Black inferiority. Black people shape-shifted to navigate that system in order to survive. That shape-shifting continues into the present.

The language of whiteness rewrites worlds and recasts people in those worlds. It reduces Black and Brown people's reality to a nonexistence—or more specifically, a noncivilized existence. Africa, Asia—they were not there in any civilized way until whiteness came, and said they were. What that teaches all of us is that our existence isn't real until whiteness names it. That makes whiteness the center, only and always, with no space for anyone else.

The language of whiteness puts anybody who is not white —men first, then women and children—on the periphery, and the periphery is the world of Blackness. Society teaches us our place. There is the periphery and the center, and the center is the goal. Being there means peace, prosperity, power, and profit. The center is whiteness, all alone, offering no room for anyone else. What that centering does is create, maintain, and sustain a rejection of your value as Black or Brown. Because who wants to be, live, love on the periphery? That's not where you thrive; it's where you rot.

White Masculinity

This language functions to create a narrative about a white masculinity, one that is win or die, rule or ruin, conquer and destroy or be conquered and destroyed. This masculinity is the benchmark for all peoples. It translates into white men ruling, white men building, and Black men ruled, Black men breaking. It is about white men who save and Black men who struggle and need to be saved. It is about white men standing tallest, strongest, most superior and pure. I say *men* intentionally, because the language of whiteness creates a white masculinity that centers white men, who they are, what they need, how they feel, that they lead, and that the rest of us are led. The white men save. Everyone else is saved. And all women serve the saviors. And it is in connection to this that emotional patriarchy exists—and must be unlearned.

That "save the world" narrative means that white men develop an emotional relationship to power and race, whereby how they feel about the world *is* the world—that's the cancer of emotional patriarchy—centering themselves to the exclusion of everyone else. That relationship is about dominion, subjugation, and exploitation. It is about how they see themselves in relation to the world. This narrative says that you, as a white man in relationship to others—all women, all Black and Brown folks—are their leader, not their brother; you are their teacher, never a student.

In other words, it is an almighty shit show—one with lethal consequences.

We're all living with the consequences of that show that manifests within systems. The consequences are front and center as we embark on and engage the work of unlearning emotional patriarchy as part of racial repair and leading toward racial healing. Here's the good news!

We Uphold Systems; We Can Dismantle Them

Systems are built by people, sustained by people, and dismantled by people. That is our work—the dismantling. That dismantling is where the racial reckoning, racial repair, and racial healing happen. We are the dismantlers we have been waiting for. That's the good news.

We too often think of systems as outside us, as a place we travel to, work at, and then leave. But systems work through us; they show up in relationships, be they professional, educational, financial, political, or religious. This means that our emotional work can contribute to structural change. Thinking that systems are outside us makes us believe we are powerless to dismantle them, but systems are upheld by us, and because they are, we do have power to dismantle them. This is where individual action connects to institutional change, to this dismantling, and it is how our emotional work can contribute.

Professional Intimacy: How Does Emotional Patriarchy Manifest?

Lena Dunham shows how a woman upholds, through intimacy, this narrative of whiteness manifest in white masculinity. Dunham is an award-winning American woman writer, actress, and creator of the HBO show *Girls*, a series about a group of white women navigating their twenties.

Murray Miller was a white male writer on the show. Dunham describes him as a dear, supportive friend, who had affirmed her, her work, and the show. Aurora Perrineau was a Black actress on the show. She alleges that Murray Miller raped her when she was seventeen. The accusation became public in 2017, during the height of the #MeToo movement founded by Tarana Burke. Women from the world of entertainment were stepping out, coming forward, and courageously naming powerful white men in the entertainment and media industry who had abused, exploited, sexually assaulted, and raped them—and faced no consequences. Dunham was one of those women. She is a survivor of sexual assault by a powerful white man in the entertainment industry. She describes herself as a fierce feminist.

Dunham intimated that Aurora was a liar and released a public statement defending Miller on Twitter. She wrote, "I believe in a lot of things, but the first tenet of my politics is to hold up the people who have held me up, who have filled my world with love, and in this case, this accusation belongs to the 3% who make false accusations."

Dunham was then subjected to fierce critique across social media for her defense of an alleged rapist—this white man in power. In response, Dunham went on to pen an apology in the *Hollywood Reporter*. She wrote, "It's painful to realize that, while I thought I was self-aware, I had actually internalized the dominant white male agenda that asks us to defend it no matter what. Something in me still feels compelled to do that job; to please, to tidy up, to shop-keep."

What Dunham describes is how intimacy allows the language of whiteness to flourish. This is what it looks like to live it and manifest it. Lena is upholding that white masculinity narrative that requires white women to believe, bolster, and be there. Her words: "internalized the white male agenda." Her work:

* To defend
* To please
* To tidy up
* To shop-keep

The person with whom she was doing that work is in her professional and personal world. She demonstrates how she rides for this language of whiteness in these two places that intersect, at the expense of a young Black woman who, like her, is a survivor, and who, like her, is navigating the particular power dynamic of a shared industry.

It's about Your Relationships, Not Your Politics

Lena's progressive politics of believing women and of feminism is no refuge for, or protection from, the emotional weight of the language of whiteness on how you navigate the world. It is a crucial reminder that your ideology is no match for your emotionality, and that doing the political work is not the same as doing the emotional work. That's why learning an Emotional Justice love language invites us to privilege the emotional, not center the political. Learning an Emotional Justice love language is about doing emotional labor.

In Arlie Hochschild's 1983 book, *The Managed Heart*, emotional labor is defined as managing your own emotions as required by certain professions. In the more recent 2018 *Fed Up: Emotional Labor, Women, and the Way Forward*, white American author Gemma Hartley writes, "Emotional labor is rooted in our relationships in a way that seems unshakable."

And yet shake up those relationships you must. Not shake up just your relationship with one white man but your role in upholding this white masculinity, as millions of white women must. This has always been your work to do, particularly as white women progressives who claim a commitment to justice and antiracism.

Looking into the eyes of the white men in your life and choosing intimate reckoning will, of course, be hard. Your relationships are places of comfort and care, of protection and provision, of upholding and being upheld. Learning this Emotional Justice love language will feel like loss—namely, the loss of a particular love for and by the white men in your life. What you gain, however, is humanity, an antiracist practice, and a more equitable world.

The real mistake is to believe that you access any of this without sacrifice or serious challenge. It will feel like trauma; it may not feel transformative at all. Not at first. "We are in each other's lives. We are dependent on each other emotionally and economically. We are in intimate, emotional, familial, sexual connection with each other. Asking women to identify as our oppressors the men we love and need is an incredibly hard ask," said Rebecca Traister, a *New York Times* bestselling white feminist author speaking about the relationship between white women and white men.

And yet ask we must. Ask we do.

An additional challenge white women face is one of incentive. So many women—especially white progressives—expect to be incentivized to show up and do their emotional work to build the world that their politics suggest they believe should exist. The issue of incentive is about white women not wanting to feel personally maligned or indicted about racism, and requiring Black people to reassure them accordingly, but that stops white women from doing their emotional work. It is manipulative, and cannot be allowed to stand.

You might think that if you believe in this world, then you fight for it, fight for what you believe. What too many are asking—and often demanding—is that Black people do the emotional labor of affirming, applauding, and appreciating out loud and in myriad ways white women's efforts to make change, and offering their gratitude that white progressives are showing up at all. This is the legacy of a racial healing model that centers whiteness, white folks' feelings, and white folks' emotional connection to race. This is not racial healing. It is historical inequity manifest as the emotional masquerading as healing.

Proximity Is Your Power: Private Intimacy

Bryan Stevenson is the author of the award-winning *Just Mercy* and whose TED talk is "The Power of Proximity." He says, "We need to position ourselves in the places where there is despair." For white women, it is the white men they are in intimate relationship with who are the cause of so much despair, but who are rarely challenged by—or even seen by—white women as the "despair creators" and maintainers, especially those who are progressive.

Intimate reckoning means that you as white women need to recognize your proximity and realize that the despair causer is sipping his morning coffee sitting across from you at the kitchen table. It is your proximity to that masculinity that provides you with conditional protection—you preserve the narrative of masculinity and evade the consequences of harm you cause Black and Brown people. It also provides a certain power over Black and Brown peoples that can be abusive and has been historically lethal. It also punishes you because this narrative is about control—not just of Black and Brown bodies but of your bodies as white women too.

For so long—for too long—you've weighed the power and the punishment, and continued to choose the power no matter the cost and consequence. Your emotional relationship to that power and how it is wrapped in whiteness offers both a sense of self in connection to white men and authority in connection with Black people. Because this is where it manifests, it is where the scrutiny, the work, the change must happen. It is here that your private intimacy rules and reigns—and ruins.

Making That Change–
Practicing Intimate Reckoning

What might unlearning emotional patriarchy and replacing it with intimate reckoning look like? Lena Dunham wrote, "My job now is to excavate that part of myself—the part compelled to please, tidy up, to shop-keep—and to create a new cavern inside of me."

And this is what intimate reckoning is about: undoing white women's emotional connection to whiteness and white masculinity, and undoing the profit and power they derive from that connection. What does that undoing look like?

Stop defending

Stop pleasing

Stop tidying up

Stop shop-keeping

Those are the key practices in unlearning this narrative of whiteness and beginning to practice intimate reckoning. These practices are the as yet undone emotional labor for white women with white men.

Redefine Emotional Labor

Gemma Hartley defines emotional labor as a "time consuming, mentally challenging, practiced skill that manifests as caring, problem solving, and emotion regulation—often all at the same time. We do it at home, at work and out in the world." Those who do it "never get a break from their role of catering to the needs of those around them."

Defining and doing emotional labor differently is what intimate reckoning requires, and what Emotional Justice and racial repair demand, and do. This is what that looks like in practice:

- Engage time to develop the unpracticed skill of letting go of tidying up, defending, and shop-keeping to affirm and please toxic white masculinity.
- Share that practice with your white sisters.
- Emotionally challenge yourselves and them.
- Step in, step up, speak out when defending, tidying up, and shop-keeping the language of whiteness manifest as white masculinity.

The Challenge

- That you will stumble and fall down
- That you will grieve
- That you will struggle
- That it will be hard (at first)

The Result

- Engaging in life-changing effort
- Changing your intimate personal and professional worlds
- Creating a well-being practice that centers humanity, not toxic white masculinity
- Practicing Emotional Justice accountability
- Contributing to creating a more equitable world

To learn this Emotional Justice love language and practice intimate reckoning, you'll need tools. The primary tool is a *circle of willingness*. This is a private space for a group of white women to share, vent, exchange, get inspired, and gather fuel to return to doing intimate reckoning. Return you must. This is long-game work.

White Men:
A Challenge, a Change, and a Chance

Here's what white women face: Why would white men unlearn the language of whiteness? It privileges them. It profits them. Here's what white women must confront: white men wouldn't do this unlearning without challenge or incentive. Here's the simple truth, and what white women must realize: you need to own and exercise your emotional power. White men cannot continue to dominate unless white women continue to join them in speaking the language of whiteness. They need your compliance to maintain their dominance.

In white men's emotional relationship to power and race, they are "the boss." The boss is always to be given the benefit of the doubt, always to be applauded and affirmed. "Boss" is way more than a title; it is how you see yourself in a world built by a narrative that has taught you that this is your sole position. Always missionary, only—and forever—on top. Who would white men become if they were not "the boss"? Their humanity lies in authority, in being the boss. For progressives particularly, not brutal authority, not violent dominance. No. Nice authority and nice dominance.

Let's be clear. This is not about a political understanding of power sharing. Lots of white men—especially progressives—get that, want that, articulate and ideologically believe that. Power sharing, which is what our humanity requires, is not about political positions with white men. So, any political or ideological argument—however well constructed, data informed, historically sound, or morally righteous and rigorous—will have little sway. That is because the language of whiteness shapes an emotional relationship to power and race. And when it comes to that emotional relationship, it is not about politics—it's about essence. It is who you are, your manhood, your idea of yourself, how you see yourself in the world and how you are seen. Emotionality is not dismantled with ideology.

Toxic Masculinity

Gemma Hartley writes that doing emotional labor would allow men to "lean into their humanity in new ways. They can step into roles that break free from toxic masculinity, live in a place of deep connection, and feel truly unafraid as they help us fight for a more equal world."

Now, to be clear, there may be elements of toxic white masculinity that many men would like to shed: the parts that ridicule displays of emotion, that treat vulnerability as weakness, that shame and punish boys and men when those emotions show up. Each of these are burdens that stifle humanity and murder much-needed empathy. The truth, though—and it is not one we have been willing to wrestle with—is that shedding that toxic masculinity doesn't necessarily include relinquishing their emotional relationship to power and race, which is about being dominant, superior, and the single authority. I mean, if you're asking white men to tweak a li'l, that's one thing. We have a multimillion-dollar industry of tweaking; it's called "diversity." But if you're asking them to transform—which is what racial repair and healing require— that's world changing, for all of us. For white men, that is soul changing.

Too many white men are willing to make change as long as that change doesn't change *them*. The language of whiteness teaches and enshrines that they—white men—are by default the solution, and therefore never the problem, never the issue. So they're not the ones who need changing.

Except, they are.

Emotional Patriarchy: White Men's Emotional Relationship to Power and Race

White men's emotional relationship to power is what entrenches and sustains inequity. That's because white men hold so many positions in leadership and because white women fail to challenge that relationship. White men hold hiring and firing power—the financial purse strings—and they wield that power when threatened. Power allows the consequences of feeling challenged to manifest in the professional, institutional, political, criminal, and personal worlds. White men, through this white masculinity, can play emotional power politics if their position feels threatened. That's what makes emotional patriarchy lethal—it's a weaponizing of the emotional using the power a person wields.

To create a more equal world, to do effective racial repair work, requires white men to change their emotional relationship to power and race. Fighting for a more equal world will feel to them like losing their leadership, which feels like losing their essence, losing themselves. Lost white men—without position or power—that's how they will feel. And that will feel like threat. It will feel as though war has been declared on their person. As though something has been taken. It will feel personal and will be taken personally. So they will fight back. Hard.

They already have.

The 2016 election, and then the 2020 election that brought an end to the forty-fifth US presidency, is a specific example. That presidency was upheld by millions of white people, and specifically white women—all protecting the language of whiteness. And as Lena Dunham reminds us, it is the emotional connection to that language that is especially powerful. This means there is no place for progressive white women to point and kiki at those who voted for the forty-fifth president.

The—predominantly—white men who scaled the US Capitol walls on January 6, 2021, in scenes of violence, lawlessness, and the whitest of white rage, were first dismissed as "knuckleheads" by Seamus Hughes, deputy director of the George Washington University program on extremism. "Knuckleheads"—a word you might use to chastise a fourteen-year-old boy who is misbehaving. Research by the Chicago Project on Security and Threats from the University of Chicago revealed that they were not. They were "regular white men"—lawyers, architects, doctors, business owners.

Adult white men, middle-aged, middle class, employers, business owners with families, stormed the site of America's political center—and were dismissed as knuckleheads. The language of whiteness infantilizes white men, and in so doing diminishes the harm they've caused, and excuses them from the tables of accountability. We teach children that there are consequences for hurtful, harming actions. White masculinity is taught—and then manifests—in white men who teach and expect that there are incessant rewards for their actions, and zero penalties. That is powerfully laid out in Ijeoma Oluo's important work *Mediocre: The Dangerous Legacy of White Male America*.

Regular white men. Regular dudes. Confronted by the narrative of not being winners, but of having lost, of being the losers. The implication of that loss on who they are as white men ignited fear that manifested as fury, in scenes that horrified and traumatized.

This issue of loss, threat to identity, and repercussions also manifests in the critical race theory furor all across America. Critical race theory (CRT) is an academic theory that applies to the world of law, and is a call to put that world in the context of race and gender. It has become the lightning rod that has created what's being described as culture wars, with calls for book bans that drag us all back to scenes from a 1930s black-and-white movie.

I have seen TV segments where critics of CRT are challenged about their objection to it. My friend Marc Lamont Hill, host on the Black News Channel (BNC), has eviscerated guests who are opponents of CRT revealing that they basically have no idea what it is. What strikes me in all these interviews is that the guests are not making arguments about CRT. They're revealing how CRT threatens their identity, the narrative of whiteness that makes them world savers, builders, and conquerors. Context cripples this delusion. And white men weaponize their emotions and mechanize institutions of power in support of their feeling threatened—this is emotional patriarchy on fleek.

I do not suggest that the weakness of their arguments should not be called out; that is a crucial part of demonstrating that their objections to CRT are about something else. I do think that their poorly formed arguments and their objections to CRT suggest that this is about reckoning with the emotional connection to whiteness and the delusional notion of world-conquering white people that shapes their identity. Violence is the love language of whiteness, so a threatened identity is treated with a marshaling of the troops to go to war against that threat.

And this does not apply only to the US. Brexit in the UK is another example. Brexit was about the withdrawal by the UK from the European Union. The UK was a part of the European Union for forty-seven years and is the only nation in Europe to leave it, doing so in January 2020. Brexit was described as a political choice for the UK either to remain as part of the European Union or to become a single, separate entity. In a world that is increasingly interdependent, the choice seemed stark and political, with economic consequences. It was not.

The pro-Brexit campaign was cast as a fight to protect Britishness, your white manhood, your value as a white working man in Britain, threatened by foreign entities. Your vulnerability as a man was at stake, and those stakes were the result of the presence of people who didn't look like you. Brexit's campaign was drowning in emotional patriarchy. It was deeply personal, about a white masculinity born of this language of whiteness and a story of a status that only stands if it stands alone. Brexit, via white masculinity, won. Britain—everyone else—lost.

Political Intimacy

Emotional patriarchy in the world of governance flourishes through political intimacy. Political intimacy manifests in how white women use their vote. It is weapon and shield. White women do not necessarily vote according to policy position, persuasive argument, or problematic stance. All three exist, and pundits articulate how confused and confounded they are that such-and-such issue didn't matter in the polls. Political intimacy is a weapon wielded with emotional clarity.

The language of whiteness flourishes via this political intimacy that consistently sides with sustaining the white masculinity that emerges from this narrative of whiteness in which white masculinity is, and saves, the world. Because of that, white women are not voting against their interests; rather, they are declaring that their interest is in sustaining the language of whiteness that enables their men to not simply function but flourish. That's where the emotional connection to power and whiteness is sustained in the political world—and that's where it must be severed.

The binary of the language of whiteness is a cancer that teaches a masculinity that says if you don't win, you're a loser, and if you're a loser you're not a man, and if you're not a man—what use are you? The language of whiteness goes to the heart of identity, and that is why the reckoning is intimate for white women. So the way millions of white women use their vote reveals the consistently misunderstood power of the emotional wrapped in the political. White women choose proximity to power, not progress for people—people including themselves, and their own bodies. The 2020 local elections in the US reveal that, and the white women who voted for Brexit reveal that too.

Political intimacy is the means by which white women protect the emotional patriarchy in governance. It is where the political manifests as the emotional, and it is a space of power wrapped in politics, but working through emotionality. Political intimacy is not about policy position; it is about protecting the emotional patriarchy. And it works. Our failure to understand this leads us to use the wrong tools to reckon with it. Part of the national reckoning with the West's patriarchal roots requires recognition of the emotional.

Women vote at higher rates than men, and have done in every presidential election since 1980. The high-profile Virginia gubernatorial election in 2021 reveals how political intimacy protects emotional patriarchy, as the results came in and the expectation of a Democratic win dissipated, dwindling the gains of the Biden-Harris administration to a sobering loss.

Intellectually, power sharing through fairer governance that includes more people is deeply appealing. The emotional connection to whiteness means that it cannot be entertained. Of course, more women are running for political office. That is important, and wonderful. Also, white women have always wanted more power when it comes to white men, but the emotional connection to whiteness in white masculinity means that white men have to rule over somebody, otherwise they are not men—and if they do not feel like men, they become dangerous. Their possessing unfettered power also makes them dangerous.

Emotional labor is part of what sustains unfair structures; and a politics of cycles of progress and regress is a place where the emotional and political combine and collide to fight the language of whiteness and to protect it. It is a holy shit show. But it can be changed.

Bryan Stevenson believes that proximity is a bright guiding light for how to make change. When it comes to intimate reckoning, it is white women's proximity to white men that must be their guiding light.

Black Challenge to a Whiteness Narrative

The language of whiteness has been challenged, again and again, by Black people, and especially by Black women. Black people—so often led, supported, enabled, and organized by Black women—move worlds. From enslavement to freedom, we have challenged—and continue to challenge—the language of whiteness. We have built worlds, fought for representative power to steer our own path as Black beings, to be human in the world. All this entails unlearning the language of whiteness, and challenging this narrative of who Black people, Black women, are, and are not. All of our movements are the manifestation of a challenge to this language of whiteness.

Intimate reckoning is not a prosecution or condemnation of our work as Black people, as Black women—it is a call to white women: it is time to do yours. Progressive or otherwise, red or blue, ideologically impressive or politically problematic—these are your men, those you work with, live with, engage with, rely on, and love. Yes, the shit is messy. Hella messy. And hard. And totally fixable. White women, you can absolutely do this.

An Exchange with Dr. Robin DiAngelo

I am talking here with Dr. Robin DiAngelo, *New York Times* best-selling author of *White Fragility: Why White People Are Afraid to Talk about Race* and *Nice Racism: How White People Perpetuate Racial Harm and Racism*, to explore intimate reckoning, what that means for her personally, how she is challenged by it, but also how she recognizes its power.

Robin DiAngelo is **RDA**. Esther Armah is **EA**.

EA: Where in your own world can you see intimate reckoning that you could do? What does that look like?

RDA: When I think about the question, what comes to mind is the reality that I am very intimidated by white men. I have a deep history around white men, as a white woman, as a white girl raised by a white male father. While I can see that the intimidation comes from a place of feeling victimized, it functions in practice to have me collude with white supremacy and patriarchy. That makes sense, right, because if I am afraid to challenge white men for my own fear, my own need to feel safe, that means I'm not going to challenge patriarchy and white supremacy. And I haven't thought about it in this context. I mean I've long known that I do have to address particularly white male anger. When I picture an angry Black man, I don't have the same response to it. Perhaps I don't have the same history around it, and it's easier for me to see the bigger context when I think about Black male anger. Most of the direct oppression I have experienced has been at the hands of white men.

The values of silence, suffering, subservience, service, sacrifice—those were so deeply instilled in me. And I see the closeness to white male power is about "Here's this place we don't have to struggle . . . Here's this place where there's a current we can move in, and not against"—and so it's going to be really seductive to have that relief of attaching to that power, and soothing that power which both keeps us safe and then benefits us because then we also have an internalized sense of superiority over someone else. We're still conditioned within a hierarchy. As I thought about your questions, for me the way we talk about white women, I think the default assumption is white middle class. Because I'm working class, I think there are some class takes here. I don't think I have less racism because I was born poor, but I just learned my place in the racial hierarchy from a different class position. One of the ways I learned it was to project our class shame on to Black people . . . our dirt, literally. I was dirty. My mother was a single mom, she was sick, we lived in our car for periods of time, she couldn't really bathe us, feed us, or take care of us, and so we were physically dirty—but we were constantly told not to touch things or go places where Black people went because they would be dirty. I can look back now and see how we used Black people to realign ourselves to the dominant white culture that our poverty separated us from. So in those moments I wasn't poor anymore—I was white.

EA: What are your thoughts on white women's protection and upholding of white masculinity? Is that true for you—and how does it manifest?

RDA: When I think about the ways I was conditioned to take care of white men, the lessons come in a few different ways. One is, your value is in your value to men. Your ability to access value or resources is through white men— and your safety is in pleasing white men. And those are pretty high-level emotional investments that you're gonna have. And that maybe one of those is how you mediate your own less-than, by being more than somebody else. That you align with that power, and it gives you a lot. It gives you status, it gives you safety, it gives you value, it gives you resource. The consequences for challenging patriarchy are intense—and that means I am going to sell you out.

EA: "Sell you out" as in sell Black people out?

RDA: Yes.

EA: Safety and intimacy—talk about how the term *safety* and racism interconnect, how that term is weaponized by white women. And how has that manifest for you, and within the work you do?

RDA: What does it really come down to when white people say they need to feel safe? It's such a perversion of the true direction of historical harm. I think it's a completely invalid, illegitimate term to come out of a white person's mouth—the need to feel safe in talking about racism. Racial justice has to weigh more than your feelings of discomfort. While I was taught to see the humanity of white men, I was not taught to see your humanity. White people are not conditioned to care about, to love Black people. But white women are conditioned to love and care about white men. That's the key crux of it.

EA: Emotional Justice is such a crucial element of transforming emotional labor. Because intimacy is the institution that upholds this relationship between white women and white men, what, for you, in leaning in and doing that labor with white men—what happens afterwards with white men?

RDA: I think of one situation. There were no real consequences for me—he wasn't my employer, I wasn't gonna lose my livelihood—but I didn't wanna deal with him so I just closed off. It was a neighbor, and there was an opportunity to keep working with him; I chose not to for my own comfort. I can't say that I went back. To be honest, that would be me giving up, for my own discomfort, my own conflict avoidance, my own fear of conflict.

EA: Let's stay with that feeling of "you gave up." For millions of white women, that's true. But it's exactly here that this is the new racial healing language of intimate reckoning, of doing this emotional labor is so necessary. Inequity is held up by not doing this labor. As you move forward and you've come away from that situation—what does that look like?

RDA: I get an image of myself in a ball—like a little rounded-up ball, stewing, feeling that there was an injustice towards me, and yet it's a kind of impotent injustice. That's actually a very old feeling for me around white men, that there is something that is not just, and you are powerless to do anything about it. That's an old feeling because I am not powerless now. But that's a great example of not addressing your own issues and patterns—and that's not going to serve you in issues of racial justice.

This was about five or six years ago and I still to this day lay in bed and feel anger about this interaction and the sense of injustice. I see you are challenging me to see the part I played in it, and it was not something that was just perpetrated on me, and I chose not to do the work of allyship, by withdrawing when it got uncomfortable or difficult for me personally.

I'm pretty direct, and considered fairly confrontational, but within myself I know there are lines that I could step over that I'm not stepping over—there are lines that I avoid. It's driven by my own fear of the anger of white men. There is the reality that patriarchy is real, and white men control the institutions, and there are very real consequences also for white women. And white women are in this really interesting position—because we are both absolutely really privileged by white supremacy, but we're also oppressed by patriarchy. It gives us an incredible way in to understanding white supremacy if we use it that way. But so often our resentment about patriarchy causes us not to be able to center someone else's oppression. So I see a lot of white women centering themselves in terms of sexism, white feminism. They can't move past their own resentment about what they haven't gotten, to even imagine centering what someone else hasn't gotten if they have to give something up—at least in their minds.

EA: For you, when you think of the emotional labor you have to do with white men, what does that mean?

RDA: For me it means staying in, it's not just saying that thing or challenging that behavior—it means staying close while the recipient of that challenge struggles with that response. It means not withdrawing, not moving away, not soothing in those moments. So it's building the capacity and the stamina to stay, to do both of those things—speaking truth to power and staying connected. So often we stay connected by not speaking truth to power. Or we speak truth to power and then we run away. I'll be honest: I recognize that in myself—speaking truth to power then running away—to be safe. I do think it's the integration of both those things.

The Emotional Justice Template

Work through your *feelings*: Frustration, sadness, resentment, anger, indignation, powerful, grief, rewarding

Reimagine your *focus*: How do I speak the language of whiteness when it comes to white masculinity? Answer this question individually.

Build the *future*: Create a circle of willingness whose focus is accountability and decentering whiteness, and that resists what can be self-congratulatory book club–type discussion. There should be at least three of you. Express your relationship to whiteness, and explore what decentering white masculinity's power might look like in your places of work and learning.

Discussion Points

What would intimate reckoning look like for me?

Whom would I invite to create a circle of willingness?

Where have I tidied up, defended, and did shop-keeping of white masculinity? What change can I make by not doing that labor?

• 4 •

Intimate
Revolution

Definition and Action to Be Taken

For **Black women** globally to unlearn the language of whiteness that teaches them that their sole value is labor. For Black men to do their emotional labor in finding their way through a masculinity that is traumatized and hypersexualized by the language of whiteness, and that too often leads to pouring their untreated trauma over the bodies and beings of Black women.

Unlearning whiteness for Black women globally means redefining this relationship to labor, normalizing and culturalizing rest and replenishment. It means unlearning *emotional currency*—having your value treated like a commodity. Unlearning whiteness for Black men means breaking up both with white supremacy's definition of masculinity that creates internalized conflict and with their expectation that Black women do the emotional labor of mothering a traumatized masculinity.

Breakdown

Intimate revolution is about the emotional work of changing Black, Brown, and Indigenous women's relationship to labor, and Black men's relationship to masculinity. This emotional work for both Black women and men is deeply complicated precisely because it is a relationship.

Labor in this case is not about a nine-to-five job that ends. It's much more than work; it is about worth. It is about an emotional connection, a relationship at the intersection of history, gender, Blackness, value, violence, and worth.

Labor, Blackness, and women are a threesome, a relationship that lives and thrives from the plantation to the pandemic and beyond. This relationship means that a breakup comes with deep roots, a long history, and modern manifestations. The entangling among labor, value, and history is precisely what makes this an "intimate" revolution. And like all breakups, it's messy.

Black Women, Labor, and History

Labor. For Black women globally, this word carries weight, history, legacy. The language of whiteness made labor life, breath, and death in the systems of enslavement, colonialism, and apartheid that built and continue to shape our worlds. Your worth was measured in how much labor you could take on, how fast you could do it and with little to no rest. Do too little, and whiteness would kill you; do too much, and that labor under whiteness could kill you.

Historically, that labor was under the sun, the lash, the massa and the mistress. For you as an enslaved Black woman, a colonized one, or one navigating apartheid, labor was your calling. Whiteness worked you to death. Literally.

And that work had multiple manifestations.

Different women did different kinds of labor. Your body was capital, and then capitalized. There was the Mammy. There was the Wench. Later, there was the Welfare Queen. Each name is a narrative by whiteness that created a specific kind of labor for Black women.

The Mammy, the Wench, the Welfare Queen

The Mammy. Domestic labor. Historically, she was a Southern, large, dark-skinned Black woman who took care of white children and tended to the needs of white families. She never asked for anything in return, she never got tired, and servicing white families was pure pleasure. She was lampooned and insulted, but that never stopped her caring for white families. She was removed from her family to take care of white people's families, and that loss was hers alone to bear. She would not visibly mourn or miss her family but be totally fulfilled by looking after white children and their families. Here was a woman who had children, but was desexualized and so somehow didn't have sex. Nothing immaculate about that conception; that's the narrative of whiteness declaring desirability had a form—and it wasn't Mammy.

The Wench/Jezebel. Sexual labor. Stimulating, exciting, satiating white men's appetites. Her sole existence was to tempt and tease. Her humanity was stripped, her sexuality all-engulfing, oozing out of every pore. That meant sexual violence could not be considered violence because her screams were not connected to struggle or pain; they were about sex and pleasure. Always. Her body and being were about desire and contempt, navigating white men's deviant lust, and white women's deadly lens.

The Welfare Queen. Political labor. Undeserving, scamming, lazy users. These were do-nothing dawdlers waiting for government assistance, hungrily eyeing the hard-earned—read white—taxpayers' dollars. That was the narrative of whiteness. This Black woman was a single mother. Blamed for her self-inflicted predicament and labeled as the main reason American ghettoes were in fact ghettoes; she failed to progress. The facts? The majority of welfare recipients were white, and the majority of those who had committed welfare fraud were male. The facts did not shape the narrative. That is what the language of whiteness does: it rewrites the narrative to serve the delusion of whiteness as rightness. *Welfare Queen* was a term engaged as a weapon of the political right. It was political currency, part of political labor to score votes, courtesy of Ronald Reagan's 1976 presidential campaign. This narrative was deadly for Black women's families and family structure. This was political labor in service to a constituency of whiteness.

Your Weaponized Body

Sexualized, mammy-fied, and demonized. Your body was treated as a weapon and then weaponized against you; your Blackness a labor sentence and your humanity a no-go, a no-no, and a who-gives-a-fuck. In each of these ways, Black women were emotional currency, their identity commoditized to serve the narrative of whiteness.

This compartmentalization of Black women and their labor was about dehumanization. Because, of course, a human woman may be a combination of caretaker, sexual being, mother, provider and one who is provided for—that is humanity, that is complexity. Physical backbreaking labor held a contradictory narrative defined by whiteness. Black folk were supposed to be content, happy to be doing this labor. The narrative of whiteness imposed joy on cruelty, weaponizing the emotional to contrive this joy on Black folk doing brutal labor from stolen freedom.

Labor as Connection to Value and Worth

What makes this history and its contemporary manifestations particularly enraging, confusing, and internalized is that there was always a parallel narrative of Black women as lazy. Backbreaking, soul-aching labor by Black women was rewritten as laziness, and the two stood cheek by jowl. This "lazy Black women" narrative was part of the psychology of whiteness. What it did was nurture a connection between value and labor within Black women—part of the internalized racism. The narrative would develop an intersection with never wanting to be seen or considered as lazy, and taking on more labor to prove that you were not. You did more to prove you were worth more. Laziness historically was a death sentence. It came alive as emotional connection: your labor and your value were how you measured how you mattered. That's because how whiteness saw you, mattered.

This seeing by whiteness created a cycle of different kinds of violence: the economic intertwined with the emotional—the connection between the two. Understanding the combined toll of both must be part of this breakup, and requires scrutiny, identification, unraveling, and unlearning. This is how the language of whiteness thrives within Black women's emotionality. This emotional connection to your value as historically defined by labor was about how much you do, how much more you can do, how much you have done, how much more you are willing to do, and how valuable you are because you do it. Enduring, exhausting, unending labor.

This connection then was about a conditioning that manifests not in the labor Black women do but in the relationship to that labor—one that took root in Black women's minds and souls.

Emotional Mammies

Physical labor extended to emotional labor as part of an oppressive system. Historically, that emotional labor was crucial to navigating the violence of the time and keeping those who wielded power happy and reassured that the Black bodies they owned and controlled were content. It wasn't historically gendered; both Black men and women did this kind of emotional labor, but it has become particularly gendered—there is now the "emotional mammy." The Black woman—of any hue, shape, or size—is expected to take care of the feelings of white people, of white women and men, of all men—no matter the cost or consequence to her, her body, her well-being.

What does that mean for Black women? How does this manifest? It manifests as Black women emotionally rearranging ourselves to make space to soothe the discomfort of white people always—even when the discomfort is about harm they have caused to us. You know that phrase "There, there"—in other words, "Don't worry, I'll take care of it." It's that. It's "there-there-ology." It has meant swallowing our anger, fighting our pain, suppressing our rage, repressing our contempt, stuffing down our humanity, shoving it hard into the crevices of our bodies so that we can keep an unpeaceful peace. It means an endless reassurance to white people that all is well, that they are "good people"—even when that makes us sick emotionally—and, all too often, eventually physically. It means choking our own Black breath to let whiteness breathe.

The language of whiteness teaches Black women that we are emotional currency. Our value appreciates or depreciates according to the service we provide for white people, for whiteness as this emotional mammy. It is our expected willingness to consistently, relentlessly provide that service that is the measure of us as valuable—no matter the ask, the demand, the weight, the pain, the harm, the toll.

How Do I Speak
the Language of Whiteness?

It is in our emotional relationship to ourselves and one another that the language of whiteness reigns, rules, and ruins, and labor's legacy lives. This emotional relationship manifests in an interconnection of self-love and self-loathing inside us. It is here that a breakup must happen.

A crucial part of unlearning whiteness for Black women is asking ourselves, How do I speak this language? How do I emotionally profit from it, invest in it? What does that look like? Here's what it looked like for me.

I was a Black woman journalist in the UK. I was an executive producer on a show about Africa, and I left to become a researcher in a white media house. Climbing up the ladder in a Black space, only to climb all the way back down to get into a white space. The position was a demotion. The language of whiteness turned it into a promotion. I was at the BBC, the British Broadcasting Corporation. The biggest broadcaster in the world. Going from Black space into white space—that act turned into ladder climbing, a definition of making it. I was therefore certified a success—to me, to my family, to friends, to the world. It was major, and I loved how other people saw me and how I saw myself because I had gained access.

I did become a better journalist; I upskilled, moved from radio to television, from being a researcher to a reporter to a producer. Remember, though: I was an executive producer before I came to the BBC. So there's that. I also became a more insecure person there, much more insecure. I fought to prove myself again and again, always starting again, even if I had climbed to a role with a different title. The title may have held more power, but I did not. I was the same.

Proving myself, being constantly questioned about my ability, being gaslit, being challenged about my right to be there. I balanced better technical skills and a higher profile with discomfort, anger, constant job insecurity, vulnerability, and the veneer of professional success. I was always professionally insecure, teetering on some language-of-whiteness-made precipice, balancing, losing my balance, and trying to gain a sure footing.

In my world of journalism, the language of whiteness always maintains insecurity for Black professionals: short-term contracts, long-term interning, the temporary do not expand to the kind of permanence that makes you secure, that allows you to exhale, to breathe, to build beyond work and explore other parts of life. It is a constant navigating and negotiating for the next piece of work. My inside was in a constant state of turmoil; my outside wore the appearance of success. It was an emotional juggling act. I kept smashing into the glass ceiling of race that the language of whiteness constructs and that so many Black journalists in the UK hit.

I became increasingly bitter, resentful, and angry. And I remember staying. Because although I was not professionally secure, I was emotionally affirmed by the language of whiteness. It was a badge, a medal. I wore it, and wearing it made me feel visible and valuable to myself, my family, my community, and the rest of the world.

I stayed. Staying took me to the edge of my own principles, my own beliefs about Blackness. I remember almost selling out a group of Black boys on a documentary I was working on—putting them in harm's way by persuading them to be on camera in a documentary that would criminalize them. I pulled back at the very last minute, went to tell the organization leader not to do the interview and not to have the Black boys he was working with do it either. I explained why. He was disappointed—suspicious too. He finally asked whether there was another way this could be done. I had to explain in more detail what doing the interview would mean for his organization, for the Black boys he was working with. He listened, shrugged, and reluctantly agreed.

He, like me, saw the value of being in a documentary made by this broadcaster, what it could mean for him and for his organization. Disappointed—and honestly annoyed with me—he agreed that the boys in his organization would no longer participate. Going home that night, I stared at myself in a mirror of fragments. *Who are you becoming?* I don't think I understood how the language of whiteness communicates to us. Not then, but I do now. It sucks. I couldn't look at myself. *Who am I? Who am I becoming? What am I willing to do? What am I not willing to do?*

I left. Finally. Not in some glorious act of justice, but angry, bitter, pushed, and resentful. If I could have stayed, my quiet truth is that I would have. Unhappy, angry, insecure, vulnerable, navigating racism, yes—but I still would have stayed. The payoff of being seen as successful, of being respected and revered—of emotional profit—allowed me to bargain with my emotional health to hold on to this appearance of, this definition of, success. That's part of how the language of whiteness showed up within me. So, leaving that job wasn't hard; it was devastating. It was also the beginning of my unlearning. Leaving was a crucial step in beginning to unlearn the language of whiteness and beginning to practice intimate revolution.

That was me in the UK.

How Do Black Women Speak the Language of Whiteness?

Black women speak the language of whiteness in the way we are taught to see ourselves, and how we are seen through the eyes of the world, white people's world. It is needing white people to see us in order to know that we hold value. We don't want to admit that—we don't admit or concede that. What we are nurtured to feel is that their seeing us identifies our worth and cements our value.

Black people can see us too—they absolutely do see us too, and that matters—but it doesn't benefit us in the same way, to the same extent. Our visibility to other Black folks doesn't carry as much weight, doesn't hold the same power, doesn't affirm us in the same way. It doesn't matter to us in the way it does when white people see us. We don't admit that either. The language of whiteness is spoken in the ways white people do not see us, and therefore we become less visible to ourselves.

We could be a Black woman in academia, in the corporate world, in the entertainment industry, in the world of tech, in politics, in media, in the cocoon that is publishing, in the nonprofit world, in retail, beauty, fashion, and in the worlds of philanthropy or education. We could be a Black woman in America, in England, in Europe, in Africa. We are Black women in a world dominated by the global language of whiteness. We may shout—millions of us do—that our Blackness is our everything, it is alpha and omega. We shout that, we live that, in myriad ways. Loudly, unapologetically, with style, rhythm, and badass bass, across borders, beyond boundaries, we claim our Blackness as beauty, balm, and bad to the bone. That's what makes this unlearning complicated. For millions of Black women, there isn't a lack of love of self; this is about recognizing that the emotional connection to our Blackness is shaped by the language of whiteness.

The language of whiteness is a narrative that teaches Black women about how invaluable we are, how grateful we should be, and how little we matter—all at the same time. We are simultaneously invaluable and without value. Even if we do not see or feel that way about ourselves yet, we are shaped by the systems of the world—by schoolteachers and school buildings, by what we watch, read, and listen to, by the institutions we work in, by a religion that dominates in the form of a blue-eyed, blond-haired cross bearer. Each will teach us that speaking the language of whiteness requires being less ourselves, and that being less ourselves is our passport to expanded possibility.

This means that we must unlearn and break up with dual intersecting narratives: grind as our mother tongue and deriving our worth from how the language of whiteness sees us as Black women, shapes how we see ourselves and how we define success.

What Unlearning Whiteness Looks Like

The actions of Pulitzer Prize–winning journalist Nikole Hannah-Jones show how she is unlearning this language of whiteness and rejecting being the emotional mammy with white elite institutions.

Hannah-Jones is creator of the 1619 project in the *New York Times*. Launched in August 2019 to commemorate the four-hundredth anniversary of when the first enslaved Africans landed in Virginia, the project offered readers a new way to think about the founding of America, and specifically the contribution made by enslaved Africans—who became African Americans—to shaping America's systems and modern economy. It was visionary and groundbreaking, and it made global headlines. It was considered controversial, and it attracted the ire of the political right.

That controversy manifested in the world of academia when Hannah-Jones applied to her alma mater, the University of North Carolina (UNC), to become the Knight Chair of Race and Investigative Journalism. It is a tenured position, and she would have been the first Black woman—and first Black person—to hold it. Tenure is the ultimate job security within academia, ensuring your freedom, your paycheck, and a certain power. She went through the rigorous interview process, and was successful. But UNC declined to give Hannah-Jones tenure . . . for a tenured position. There was public uproar. Across social media, academics lambasted what happened to her; think pieces were written; cable news did segments. The pressure, national scandal, and weeks of protest led UNC to—finally, reluctantly—offer her tenure. She said no, declining their offer with an eight-page letter and a television interview with CBS anchor Gayle King.

Hannah-Jones explained to King that although the position was supposed to be tenured, when the university failed to offer her what every other Knight Chair had been given, she said yes to a five-year contract without tenure. She explained, "It was embarrassing to be the first person to be denied tenure. I didn't want this to become a national scandal; I didn't want to drag my university through the pages of newspapers because I was the first—and the only Black—person in that position to be denied tenure. So I was willing to accept it. I never spoke up during that time."

Her initial response is how the language of whiteness is spoken—the sometimes quiet acceptance of injustice to avoid the professional consequence of speaking up. It's spoken here in privileging a white institution's reputation over Hannah-Jones's individual reality. Speaking that language meant rearranging herself to accommodate the school's discrimination, its injustice done to her—and protecting the school with her silence. No shade, no judgment. It's something millions of Black women do, have done—probably without the same global scrutiny—but nevertheless, we have done it, and continue to do it.

Hannah-Jones wrote in her resignation letter, "For too long Black Americans have been taught that success is defined by gaining entry to and succeeding in historically white institutions. For too long, powerful people have expected the people they have mistreated and marginalized to sacrifice themselves to make things whole."

In the interview with Gayle King explaining her decision, Hannah-Jones said: "Since the second grade when I started being bused into white schools, I have spent my entire life proving that I belonged in elite white spaces that were not built for Black people. I decided I did not want to do that anymore. This is not my fight. It's not my job to heal the University of North Carolina. That's the job of the people in power who created the situation in the first place."

And it is here that unlearning the language of whiteness occurs. A Black woman saying that it is not her job to heal a white institution is refusing to be an emotional mammy, all in real time. She is no longer privileging the white narrative over her own emotional well-being. She is choosing herself, opting for an emotional safety and rejecting becoming the institution's emotional mammy.

What Nikole Hannah-Jones did is big, because Black women's emotional labor is always expected to cater to whiteness no matter the cost or consequence to our Blackness, our being, and how it may bury us.

Gayle King asked the pivotal question we Black women must all ask ourselves when it comes to unlearning whiteness and beginning to practice the Emotional Justice love language of intimate revolution: "What is the personal toll this has taken on you? How has this affected you personally?"

Hannah-Jones responded, "It's been extremely difficult. People see me as a symbol of things they love or they hate. But I'm a human being."

This is the crucial step—by acknowledging our own humanity, our own breaking point, and by privileging our well-being, we unlearn the language of whiteness and actively begin the practice of intimate revolution—we are reimagining our relationship to labor, whiteness, and our humanity.

Black Women's Labor for Freedom

Black women's labor globally was also in service of freedom, of holding agency over their own bodies and fighting tooth and nail for self-ownership and actualization. It matters that we honor and name that. Black women absolutely did that. Every independence movement—from civil rights and women's rights in the US and the UK, to independence in Africa, to fighting apartheid in South Africa—reveals how Black women's labor was also, and always, about freedom fighting, a warrior spirit, and a resistance to being named and known solely according to the language of whiteness.

Black women have always had to be fluent in multiple narratives in order to make our way through a world whose dominant language is whiteness. That means we are creatively, culturally, intellectually, artistically, and musically literate beyond whiteness, even as we are simultaneously nurtured, traumatized, and shaped by it. It is that combination that births complexity and contradiction.

We built worlds before whiteness rebuilt them in its image and likeness—destroying ours. We built movements that have consistently challenged white men's notion of themselves as authorities with dominance over our bodies.

We—Black women and Black men—are the Black frontline across communities, cities, countries, and continents. It is our fight, our willingness to stare down the violent face of white supremacy that is the foundation of freedom movements. That is our global truth. This Emotional Justice love language, though, is not about that unequivocal truth.

The Black Community's Warriors

Black women are the designated warriors—and worriers—about the state of the Black community. We are its caretakers, nurturers, service providers. We are its first responders. There is a beauty and a badassness to that role, one that we revel in and are rewarded by. There is power and progress because of that work. Black women are builders, believers. There is change because of that work. There is deep love in this too. When the arc of the world bends toward justice, it is because Black women are the arc.

But we are not bending. We are breaking.

Being the arc without sufficient support and without a strategy for rest and replenishment is part of the community labor landscape. That landscape must change for our individual health, communal health, and societal health, for a practice of liberation.

Grind. That's the contemporary manifestation of this historical relationship to labor birthed by the language of whiteness, and its legacy. *Grind* is not a word for Black women; it's our Black mother tongue. It's a culture, a generational inheritance passed down, passed around, and emerging from the bellies of Black women the world over. It is toil always, rest never, reward rarely. We grind for good, we grind for God, we grind for men. No healing lies there.

I call it *push-through-o-nomics*. Grind ignores every sign that your body, spirit, and mind cannot do any more, take any more, or move any more. It demands that you discard all those signs and push through—and find power and pleasure in pushing through, even after you have broken. Breaking is illegible, unacceptable, and makes you somehow less of a Black woman. It is familiar unrelenting exhaustion. Your heart aches, your soul is breaking, your health is failing; don't stop . . . even if it's killing you, if you're burned out and burned up—but keep pushing, keep going, you must, you have to, keep going. Always, keep going.

Black women are the caretakers. Who takes care of the caretakers? They must. We must. And that is what intimate revolution invites us to learn. This is not about prosecuting Black women's agency, endurance, and sheer will and fight to survive. We are here because of that. But this is about Black women's healing. So it is not about toughness. It's about toll, the devastating toll on who we become as a result of the language of whiteness and the toll of unrelenting resistance.

Unlearning is hard because this language of grind envelops and surrounds us—our mothers, grandmothers, our girls, our families, our communities, our men, the organizations for which and in which we work, in which we serve—but that do not always serve us—each and all of these communicate and demonstrate how grind is gangsta and glorious. It is expected and required.

Black women have created emotional codes and systems to essentially keep each other speaking push-through-o-nomics. We can be emotional litigators of one another if we stop speaking it. We police one another with our "Get it together" mantras designed to bolster, but that breathe deadly "You better not break" vibes. Designed to help, they harm. They are part of a historical inheritance, part of the untreated trauma.

There is a growing movement around "radical rest," connecting rest to revolution, divesting from capitalism, and engaging Black women in exploring this. Important work by organizations like the Nap Ministry, founded by Tricia Hersey, use social media to articulate crucial messages of rest and replenishment. Hersey expands on this need for rest, its origins and context with important work in her book, *Rest Is Resistance: A Manifesto*.

To not battle through, to stop, to choose rest, and to privilege replenishment trigger deep feelings of guilt. We emotionally back-and-forth within ourselves, questioning and then challenging our own feelings, talking ourselves out of them, guilting ourselves because of them. Often, perhaps eventually, we convince ourselves that we "deserve rest, dammit"; we even justify rest, but too often we're unpersuaded by our own internal need and pushed by ancestral inheritance. We find ways to push through, and keep going.

For the Love of Black Men

Between Black women and Black men there is a particular emotional labor—the emotional grind—that is a complicated, deep abiding love. Black men are the loves of Black women's lives. There is such beauty and depth and power in that love. The language of whiteness and the legacy of untreated trauma from our history mean that the love shows up in ways that can wound, that harm liberation and threaten emotional freedoms.

Black masculinity born of the language of whiteness and wrapped in racism created a complex relationship about protection, power, and harm. There is a protection by Black women of Black men; there is an expectation that this protection covers them always, in all circumstances—even when they harm and hurt. Within the Black community globally, there is an expectation that Black men are protected from the consequences of their harm. Such protection stifles humanity, stunts growth, and hurts and harms. Black women and men are one another's protectors and providers. But not in a traditional sense or space. Black women provide cover and shelter from the cancer of racism that emotionally penetrates and devastates Black men. Black women provide a mirror for some of what Black men loathe within themselves that has been shoved into them by the language of whiteness.

Black men use Black women to do their own emotional labor, to reassert a masculinity trampled on by the language of whiteness. Black women hurt, hate, love, and adore Black men for who they fight to be, and for how whiteness breaks them. Because of how the language of whiteness targets Black masculinity, and how patriarchy rolls up, squads up, and demands the center seat at every table, this love is always complicated.

In other words, this love turns into privileging Black men over the health and well-being of Black women. And that's just not good for a thriving community.

Black Masculinity, Labor, and the Language of Whiteness

The systems of oppression treated Black men's bodies like beasts—of labor, appetite, danger. They took no account of souls and hearts. Each story served a narrative and holds a legacy that has created an emotional connection to masculinity that wrestles with power—what that looks like and feels like, and how it manifests.

For Black men, intimate revolution means doing the emotional labor of navigating their masculinity. This is tender, complex, traumatized, challenging territory.

Black masculinity is shaped by the language of whiteness and, specifically, white masculinity's narrative of savior, conqueror, and civilizer. And while that narrative tells Black people that they were saved, conquered, and civilized, it offers a dual complicated narrative for Black masculinity.

The language of whiteness set a foundation for what masculinity looked like, and then within its systems of oppression stripped Black men of that foundation. White men understand their dominion in relationship to subjugation, of Black men and all women. They are on some alpha shit. Black men navigate and negotiate these complex and contradictory masculinity narratives: being a man is about having power over somebody, and that power is what communicates to you that you are a man. How do you uphold that complexity and contradiction?

Intimacy and Black Women's Emotional Labor

Intimacy. I describe it as an institution where the language of whiteness flourishes. It is an institution within Black communities too. Black men work out their masculinity through Black women's emotional labor. There is a mothering of Black men by Black women, a caretaking that is expected, that Black girls are nurtured to provide; it becomes an emotional patriarchy.

How do you feel powerful in a world that treats your body as a threat and hyperpowerful, and simultaneously infantilizes you as a man, but adultifies you as a Black boy? What is the toll on your relationship to masculinity and your Blackness with those competing narratives? Where do you figure out how to find and feel your power as a Black man?

That feeling of power is fed through relationship—the emotional figuring out is so often done for them by Black women. It is here that emotional patriarchy manifests within the Black community. It is an expectation of the privileging, prioritizing, and centralizing of Black men's feelings no matter the cost and consequences of those feelings.

Black women and men cannot take refuge in their politics to do this work. You may be the fiercest pan-Africanist, feminist, and progressive, dedicated in your commitment to each or all of these. Each matters. Each carries weight and may shape how you have come to see and understand yourself, your world, and the world. The emotional work Black women and men must do is about the emotionality of our political worlds. There is a difference between these two worlds: one is about philosophy, and this is about emotionality. And the language of whiteness takes residence in your emotional connection to, and relationship with, Blackness, shaped by white supremacy.

It does so in ways that are unshaken by having good politics, good political arguments, and sound historical analysis of the challenges of racism in a world dominated by whiteness.

You may have great politics, but that sheds no light on your emotionality. And it is in your emotional connection to Blackness that the language of whiteness wreaks havoc. The rage that can emerge comes from the simultaneous realization of how much the language of whiteness matters and manifests—even with a politics of Blackness—is painful. Anti-Blackness, we call it. Anti-Blackness is an offshoot of a narrative of whiteness; it is a manifestation of this language. It holds the power, and determines outcomes of Black life, so to be white is to hold power. Who aspires to feel powerless?

From the Plantation
to the Pandemic and Beyond

The pandemic reveals how the legacy of labor, and the long-standing inequities that labor created, continue into the present. Staying home was the way to stay safe, said the world's health experts—except for frontline workers. And who were they? Millions of Black women and men. They had to go to work. They were the front line—the black front line. Lockdown was not an option, because the historical labor that built worlds also created systems of entrenched inequity and economic disparity. Those systems made labor a place where you were paid less, had to do more, got the worst jobs, juggled to make ends meet and keep families going.

So labor and its legacy lingered, making you vulnerable during the pandemic and leading to the devastating loss of life, as revealed by the data. COVID has killed one out of every eight hundred African Americans. COVID has killed Black people ages thirty-five to forty-four at nine times the rate

of white people, with Black men constituting a dispropor-
tionate number of them. Sobering. Devastating. Generation
changing.

Unlearning Push-Through-O-Nomics, aka What Intimate Revolution Practice Looks Like

Simone Biles, the four-foot, eight-inch Black gymnast who
dazzles with strength, grace, and what-a-wow routines, is the
most decorated gymnast in the world, and has consistently
won gold medal after gold medal for America. In the 2020
Tokyo Olympics, she withdrew from the all-around women's
final, which would end with the USA claiming the silver medal
and their competitors, Russia, winning the gold.

A statement from USA Gymnastics said in part, "After further medical evaluation, Simone Biles has withdrawn from the
final individual all-around competition at the Tokyo Olympic
Games in order to focus on her mental health."

Simone said, "I say put mental health first. Because if you
don't, you won't enjoy sport and won't succeed as much as
you want to. So, it's okay sometimes to sit out the big competi-
tions to focus on yourself, because it shows how strong a com-
petitor and person that you really are, rather than just battling
through it." She explained that she had no physical injuries,
that the emotional toll is what caused her to withdraw.

It is here that Simone is rejecting push-through-o-nomics,
and laying down a generational inheritance. This is what intimate revolution looks like.

Intimate revolution is the kind of change that doesn't make
rest revolutionary; instead it is simply human, and it doesn't

require a thesis, dissertation, or a UN convening for us to honor our need to rest, to restore, to replenish. Unlearning whiteness means changing our relationship to rest, and not associating rest with laziness.

An Exchange with Dr. Jennifer Mullan

I am talking here with Dr. Jennifer Mullan, creator of DeColonizing Therapy, an awardee of the Essence Essential Heroes Awards on Black Mental Health, and a clinical psychologist working in prisons and academia for more than a decade.

Jennifer Mullan is **JM**. Esther Armah is **EA**.

EA: Unlearning the language of whiteness is complicated for us as Black women because it nurtured how we derive our worth, our value—it's complicated shit. What has that looked like for you? How have you spoken the language of whiteness in your work?

JM: I did a lot of harm. Not consciously. Many of us—prior to understanding the effects whiteness has on people of the global majority, on people of color throughout the globe—we are taught, we are trained, we are educated on this façade of Eurocentricity—what I like to call *caucasity*. I've also participated in whiteness in not being conscious of the ways I was getting the promotions, moving forward, being seen because of the way I was perceived as "less of a threat," or more "palatable" for certain audiences. I was not really looking at the ways color, identity, how my Blackness shows up, how it doesn't, how I identify, where I get to identify—all that. I know for sure that whiteness has affected all these ways. There are so many ways I found myself being a chess piece, being placed, not being aware that I was being utilized, and being tokenized. I've really had to look at how I internalized white supremacy, how the work that I do has internalized it.

EA: How did you learn about grind, and from whom?

JM: My mother. And my grandparents. My grandfather would look me in the eye and say, "You have to make sure people respect you. In order to get respect, this is what you need to do." He would say, "I'm an immigrant. My people were originally brought over to Panama without consent. We did not consent to build that [Panama] Canal. We did not consent to being taken from the shores. And so your job is to work really hard, get an education, never take a day off." In his mind, this is how he made it. And he didn't, right. They were still struggling paycheck to paycheck. He would tell me, "Don't forget who you are, and where you came from. You have to work that much harder than everybody else. They're gonna assume that you're lazy, and that you lie." He gave me this whole outline of how to grind. And I took him seriously for so long. I respected him so much, and people respected him so much. But now looking back, that [notion of grind] continued to be perpetuated by individuals that were fed the same lies. This lie that in order to be worthy, in order to be good enough, you have to grind, grind, grind. You can never stop. My mother passed that down to me. I remember falling down the stairs taking my dog for a walk and getting hurt badly—ankles bleeding, swelling—my mum wraps it all up, she's really, really tender with me. And then she's like "Let's go. Time for school." And I said, "Where am I going?" She said, "You're going to school." And I say, "What do you mean I'm going to school! I *almost died!*" But my mother said, "Let's go! And you're going to gym

class. And you're not getting out of anything." Now looking back, we talk about it. And even now, she—or I—will
say "I'm so lazy" because I'm sitting on the couch. And
then I have to check her—or a friend will check me. Is
that lazy? Or are you giving yourself some space to rest?

EA: Talk some more about the relationship we as the women
of the global majority have between grind and worth and
labor and laziness—and how they combine to make so
many of us grind harder.

JM: We were mules. We were labor. Our bodies were labor.
Our survival depended on what we could do, how well
we could do it, and how long we could bear that brunt
and that burden. I believe from continent to continent we
see that show up. We see how colonialism has continued
to rape us of our natural ways, of our rhythm of being.
I think that from the very beginning it has been about
what we could be doing for "master," for the institution
of whiteness. Across the globe we see this. There's this
notion that there's something wrong with me if I can't
keep up; there's something wrong with me if I'm feeling
burnout.

EA: How did grind shape your understanding of success, and
impact your approach and definition of being successful?

JM: With these credentials, with these initials after my name,
with this "Dr.," perhaps people would look at me differently. I would no longer be overlooked; I would no longer
be second-guessed. I think a lot of us had that feeling.
There was this illusion, this belief that I would suddenly
be free of various types of discriminations and microag-
gressions. And again, it wasn't conscious—I wasn't saying,
"Oh, I won't be discriminated against because I have these
letters after my name." It was a sense of things will just

be easier, I would have more freedom, I won't be getting questioned and insulted about things. I won't have to deal with all these types of isms. And it affected my worth deeply. Some of my identity got tied up in that. And I feel like I am still untangling myself from that violence.

EA: How did your identity get tied up in that?

JM: I was leaving the university I'd been working in for the last twelve years. When I put in that letter, I was singing around the campus. I wasn't prepared for all of the material that I had—inadvertently or not—pushed down for later within my own self and identity. It was particularly around productivity, around my self-worth, around this martyr archetype of "I'm helping, I'm worthy," regardless of how bone-tired I am, how it's affecting my interpersonal relationships, how I've witnessed myself not being able to show up for people that I love in my life—because of my job. So, when I left the institution, I embarked on this really dark period. I really think that the grind—white-bodied supremacy—really took me for a loop. I wasn't the only one. A friend of mine—a Black woman—said to me, "I can't get off the couch," or "I can't get outside." I was in the same place, but embarrassed to admit it. Here we both were—on our islands of invulnerability, trying to throw a rope at each other, but still as Black women having a really hard time being honest about how we're feeling. Is this depression? Is this anxiety? What is this? Who am I? What am I to the world? Do I matter anymore if I'm not the director of this center, if I'm not a professor, if I'm not the face of this program? So, on many levels I felt "not enough." It's only been the last two or three months have I been able to put language to this. I'm working through that—that I am enough, that I am worthy, that I'm allowed to set boundaries. I'm allowed to ask for what I need.

EA: Let's talk emotional mammies. It's an Emotional Justice term. It's when women of the global majority are expected to take care of the feelings of white people—white women, all men—no matter the cost or consequence to their being, their body, no matter the harm. What did it look like for you?

JM: I have to take a breath, because I felt that. I always felt like I was stepping on eggshells, and I was always taking care of white people's feelings. Always. I would be activated, triggered, irritated; I felt the audacity, the level of narcissism. I felt like I had to be strategic all the time. I constantly felt drained. I've been on medical leave three separate times, done kickboxing for my rage. I nearly died multiple times, dehydration in the hospital, my body was shutting down. I had surgery, so I had to be out for the summer. I always woke up—after eight or nine hours of sleep—tired, depressed. And I would be on my way to work and I would start sobbing. I could name all the ways I was Humpty Dumpty trying to put myself back together again—I wasn't the problem. We're not the problem.

EA: Intimate revolution, unlearning whiteness—what does that look like for you and your work?

JM: For me, intimate revolution is about taking a lot more time. It's about coming back into my body, and making a promise that I'm going to slow down, because I'm more creative on that second and third day. When I slow down, and I don't pick up too many calls and try to be the hero martyr—something I do to myself—then I'll be a better friend, partner, and I have more space for myself. When we start to slow down, step back—I can choose to live in joy, to step into my body, check in with myself, take care of myself before I give parts of myself to everyone. For me, that intimate revolution is about looking at how to hold myself and those I love, lovingly accountable. Not what whiteness has told us is fair, but looking at how I operate my business, and leaving space for the emotional needs as well. I am going to need that kindness, and I have needed that kindness before. I owe it to myself and my ancestors to set boundaries, and I'm entitled to do that. My hope is I continue to call myself in lovingly, in questioning grind culture and in realizing grind culture is another way to enslave us. Only white supremacy wins when the rest of us are grinding.

The Emotional Justice Template

Work through your *feelings*: Guilt, frustration, resentment, anger, rage, reward, grateful

Reimagine your *focus*: How do I speak the language of whiteness when it comes to labor and my sense of value? How has speaking this language of whiteness shaped how I work and how I feel about success?

Build the *future*: Centering intimate revolution and emotional well-being as part of a sustainable work life

Discussion Points

Where did you learn about grind? What impact did that learning have on you?

What would intimate revolution look like for you?

• 5 •

Resistance Negotiation

Definition and Action to Be Taken

For white women and white men committed to action in pursuit of racial justice to work through the discomfort of the feelings of being maligned and indicted, of your insides that squirm, protest, deny, and defend as you are challenged about race, harm, and change. You want to flee. Don't. Your instinct is to deny. Stop. Your trauma is triggered. Pause.

Your historical reaction to manufacture danger, fear, and tears is at 100. Stare each of these in the face and tell yourself to *stand down*. You are in negotiation with your resistance. Inequity stays when you leave; this is about learning to stay when you're struggling, as a major part of unlearning the language of whiteness. You are replacing the emotional economy with resistance negotiation—learning a love language to navigate through white fragility.

Breakdown

Resistance negotiation is about identifying the difference between being attacked and needing to defend yourself versus feeling attacked because you're being challenged about an issue of race and racism. The difference matters. The former may be about life or death. The latter is about the work required to effectively practice healing as you navigate through what you feel is a racial reckoning, but is actually the act of unlearning the language of whiteness. What you are doing is setting aside the emotional economy and stepping into your emotional work.

Resistance negotiation is about dealing with a history of manufactured attack. I say "manufactured" because, of course, being challenged is not being attacked. Having your power challenged, behaviors challenged, accountability challenged are all part of what must happen for us to develop a racial healing practice. It's not magic. It's the 3 Ps of Emotional Justice—path, process, practice.

The language of whiteness has created a false narrative of whiteness as the best and anything not white as a problem needing fixing. We must all deal with that narrative. For white women and white men, one way it manifests is as feeling attacked when you are being challenged about issues of race and racism. That's rooted in a history where to be challenged by someone who is Black is heinous, illegal, and a total disrespect for what is delusional white superiority. It comes with consequences that would often be violent for the Black person. That may involve losing something that is crucial to that person's well-being or livelihood; it may even result in death. That is history. That history has legacy. That legacy has consequences. That legacy manifests in contemporary exchanges about race and racism.

Let's move through this. Historically, the consequences of challenging white people were life threatening for Black people. Today, the consequences can manifest in an abuse of power by white people toward those doing the challenging.

Your Emotional Connection to Whiteness

We are now at the heart of messiness for white women and white men committed to justice. That is because your progressive ideology probably agrees intellectually with system dismantling, power being challenged, and even power sharing. But it is your emotional connection to whiteness and power that is being challenged and that requires dismantling. This is the crux. Resistance negotiation is actually an unlearning of your emotional connection to whiteness, power, and race. It's not about Black and Brown people and racial justice.

What you are wrestling with is your relationship to resistance. It's a negotiation that you must learn to engage in. There are two steps to name and recognize.

The first step is to name resistance as manufactured fragility. Dr. Robin DiAngelo's *New York Times* best-selling book *White Fragility* explores how being challenged about race is triggering. We've created feel-good-ology vocabulary that once again centers the discomfort of whiteness. What we need is honesty. Truthfully, there isn't a way to feel good about being challenged when it comes to severing a relationship between power and whiteness, but we can absolutely feel better about doing our particular part to make change, and in so doing, redefine how systems work through us.

I challenge the notion that there is a fragility to whiteness. There is a *focus* to whiteness, one that engages the emotional to evade being accountable, one that weaponizes emotions to do that work. White progressives would like antiracism work to be joyful. Is that possible? I have no idea. I do know that I reject doing the emotional work required to figure out how to make trauma somehow joyful—frankly, it's a weird ask. Frankly, it's a whiteness-centering ask. So we should all reject it.

The second step is to pay attention to what emotions are triggered due to the challenge, to pay attention to what you do about that challenge, to wrestle with those feelings and choose a different action.

These are the two specific steps and stages in resistance negotiation. They are about moving away from manufacturing attack and therefore defending yourself by resorting to historical tactics that have repercussions for Black people. You negotiate with your resistance to do this differently, to recognize that history has you tripping, that what racial healing requires is for you to be challenged over and over again; ideas about who you have been taught you are will disappear, and what emerges is a humanity that no longer resorts to historical triggers to avoid contemporary consequences of problematic behavior.

Pause. Yup, the shit is hard. Or rather, you have no sustainable relationship to being challenged on issues of race and racism, so when you're confronted, you emotionally scurry into spaces and corners where progress has never lived, but stalling flourishes. You can no longer do that. This is what must happen instead: you learn to negotiate with your resistance. This learning is transformative for exchanges, engagements, and work toward racial healing, toward a fuller humanity.

Become the Change You Claim

When you actively negotiate with your resistance, you, and indeed your organization, stop saying things like "We are committed to an inclusive and diverse environment" when neither of those things is true. Not in practice. Not in your leadership spaces, those spaces of power where hiring and firing happens and where sustainable, transformative change that could center equity is possible, but often neglected. This is not about public statements that have too often descended into "statementism"—whereby organizations use words to convey a change that, too often, they do not make. When you defer to such statements when being challenged about harm done on issues of race and racism, you are not doing the Emotional Justice love language work of being honest about your resistance.

Because this is about an Emotional Justice love language, it is about the living culture, the practice within the spaces where you lead, live, learn, and work, and the hidden values that drive behavior. We are not starting over; we are starting with where we are, to do what we have not done: make big, hard change when it comes to whiteness.

Resist performance, resist cheering for pebble-sized steps in the eye of a tsunami and high-fiving nonexistent action as a way of sidestepping hard change. That time is gone. We no longer have the luxury of setting our racial justice clocks according to white discomfort's time zone. It has been this way for so, so long. Change cannot happen in this time zone. It is not designed to happen here. What gets done is tweak-o-nomics. Your discomfort emerges because your power is being challenged, and your instinct is to fight what you perceive as your corner being threatened. That instinct is at 100. Stare down the trauma that will be triggered as you unlearn centering whiteness, stare the discomfort dead in its face, stand down, and then *stay*.

Negotiate with yourself not to seek out Black women to deflect what is your labor, your legacy, and your work to do. This is what it means to choose Emotional Justice over privilege and comfort. This is naming your oppression as manufactured fear and emotional manipulation, and instead walking through each step: resist deflection, resist denial, resist defending, resist blaming, resist tears, and wrestle with what has been learned, tried, and tested and has functioned to stifle progress and stimulate hostile exchanges that paralyze possibility and kill progress. This is how you stay; this is how you sever the connection to whiteness and power, and stay on a road of sustainable racial healing.

An Exchange with Courtney Martin

I am talking here with Courtney Martin, a *New York Times* best-selling author and white feminist.

Courtney Martin is **CM**. Esther Armah is **EA**.

EA: Let's talk about resistance for you personally and how that has shown up for you. How has hard change shown up when you are challenged—or feel challenged—about race? What behaviors have you engaged in the past or have learned to do differently now? We're going to take a bit of a journey.

CM: The first thing that comes to mind is, in white culture, particularly America, a disconnection with your body. There's a disconnect that families breed in their kids' bodies. One of my learning curves as an adult has been learning to notice my body, and that's the first place to pay attention. Let's say I'm having a conversation with a friend. I was thinking about a conversation with a Black woman friend of mine; it was right after Trump got elected. A group of my college friends had started an organization to challenge his leadership. It was a multiracial group, but mostly white. I was mentioning it and excited about it. And she said how frustrated she was that people like my friends were getting all this funding in this moment. And in my body—because I'm starting to pay attention to my body—there was this flare-up. There was this defensiveness. And I wanted to tell her—and I think in the moment I did tell her—that this is a multiracial group, there are people of color here—and really giving her all the reasons why this is not what it looks like.

It did not go well. We got into a conflict, parted ways, and then I had to do the work of thinking through it and reflecting on my reaction and figuring out what does it look like to go back to her, and try to repair and talk to her about what happened for me, apologize, and hope for her grace. This gets back to the relationship thing—have we fed the relationship enough that she's up for giving me that grace, and hanging in there with me, and hearing my apology and doing all the things? Thankfully she is, and she was.

And so for me—the thing I'm trying to get better at is being embodied, particularly when that flare-up happens—and then ask myself about it before I have some kind of response. So for me it's body first. As a white person, learn how to be back in your body, and notice when you're getting defensive flare-up.

In the best-case scenario, I would never have said anything to her that was defending white structures of power and privilege, but sadly I didn't. So then it's how do you reflect, depersonalize, and develop your own muscles of repair and apology?

EA: Speaking about becoming embodied, one of the tools of resistance negotiation—for white women in particular—but also for white men, is what I call "discomfort muscles." Discomfort muscles are about unlearning a history where your body has always been the one that's been worshiped in different ways. When you say that white people are not in their body—I think that it's not that they are not in their body; it's that the way that they're in their body is, whatever feeling occurs is the right feeling and should not be challenged. It's the absence of expecting a human interaction—in other words, somebody's responding to how you show up in your body in a way that is a problem for them is actually an alien response for white people because the history of oppressive systems has always been that Black and Brown people have to navigate around the way white people show up in their body, for safety. It's literally been a safety mechanism. So I want to talk through this exchange with your friend and the steps of it—because there's something really instructive.

CM: The defensiveness, the explanation—I think it's rooted in the metanarrative that as a white person I want to be part of—which is, of course racism is bad, and me and my friends aren't a part of it, or me and my family aren't a part of it. This is the subconscious of white progressives—we're happy to point the finger all day at other white people, but when it's reflected back that our people—or we—are personally benefiting from these structures, there's a bit of a backlash. Because the response is "Oh no, I walk around all day with this narrative about myself," and so the defensiveness is "Oh no, you must have it wrong," because that would shatter my narrative—that I'm one of the good ones, one of the good white people.

EA: And that narrative is about your politics, your ideology. With Emotional Justice, I always say it's not about your political sophistication or your ideological conviction; it's really about an emotional connection to whiteness and power about race that is rooted in a history that really needs to be healed—that hasn't been healed. White progressives use political arguments to engage what is actually emotional. The reason there will always be a disconnect is that they have nothing to do with each other. You can be as ideologically sound, philosophically pure, and as politically progressive as a person can be, but that has nothing to do with who you are in the world as a human being when it comes to your connection to race and whiteness, because that has to do with soul and essence and fear—and how much white supremacy is rooted in ideas of subjugation and exploitation and dominion. So you may know politically and philosophically that this is wrong, but that doesn't mean the emotional connection to that is automatically unlearned. And so the instinct, the flare-up, is the emotional connection to whiteness manifesting, making itself heard in very specific ways.

Walk through that differently, step back, and look at that again—what would be the walkthrough? What would be the response to your emotional flare-up— which is literally what resistance negotiation asks you to wrestle with? You're navigating that internal bodily response when somebody is challenging you about a particular issue.

CM: I think the more that I put myself into situations, whether that's interracial friendship or multiracial organizing, or getting feedback from Black writer friends, or anywhere the flare-up happens[, the stronger this muscle gets]. It's a muscle for me of noticing and talking with my body at that moment, and the more that I have those experiences with being challenged—having my worldview challenged or having my identity challenged in some way, the more practice I have of being "Oh, there's that feeling." And this gets back to discomfort and my ability to sit with it. Because of the way I've structured my life and the kinds of people that I have been attracted to, and the communities

I'm a part of, now I have plenty of opportunities for this kind of discomfort—and that's great, because that just means I get better and better and better at noticing. Either it lowers because the flare-ups get less intense, or I can say I'm feeling this, "Ah, okay, I know what this is"—and I just keep moving. Or I just get better and better at talking to it and hanging in there. I think for me it's about a pause. If I were to have that conversation over again with that friend where I'm feeling "Oooh, that hurt," and I feel bad.

EA: Part of how whiteness is protected is by segregating itself—and that segregation manifests in policies and every part of politics that seeks to maintain division in order to create a cocoon—a false cocoon of this purity space. And so what makes the love languages really important is that they are about communities sharing the language with each other in order to make change within their own communities. And so while, for example, white people segregate from people of color, they're not segregated from other white people. And a really specific part of the resistance negotiation—particularly for white progressives—is about doing the work with other white people specifically about this . . . and engaging different kinds of conversations because they do have proximity. And the question is, how are they using their proximity to whiteness?

I know Bryan Stevenson talks a lot about proximity to vulnerability, and in the Emotional Justice love languages, we say that the proximity that white women have is to other white women and white men. So that's where the work has to happen. The mistake is to imagine that it happens by having more proximity to Black people, because that's not where the change needs to happen, and that's not where the challenge needs to happen, it's not where the unlearning needs to happen.

CM: What strikes me about what you just said is with my friend the discomfort is spontaneous, it's in the moment, it's not something I chose—it's we're having this relationship and we're having this conversation—and then all of a sudden this happened. In whiteness, if I'm talking to my husband, or if I'm talking to another white mother, I have to choose the discomfort. The comfort is there—if a white mom says something about the chaotic, rough school in our neighborhood, I can very much choose the comfort of nodding my head and sipping my coffee and saying nothing. Or saying something really bland that doesn't truly address the issue, and is probably not going to offend her, like "Oh, you know—you should take another look at that school"—or I could choose the discomfort of saying something direct like "I see that as coded, racist language." And so, in the interracial scenario, you have the discomfort as a white person, and in the white scenario you have to choose the discomfort, which is a pretty high bar. I choose it a lot because that's who I'm being in the world. But it strikes me that no wonder we don't do the work more because it strikes me that you have to pursue the discomfort.

EA: This notion of choice—of what you choose and what you don't—it is at the heart of resistance negotiation. Because you're also really negotiating with your own comfort, you're negotiating with your own instinct to choose safety rather than struggle. And you're negotiating with your instinct to stay silent. And in Black communities when people are navigating particular issues, the difference is because the world is racist and there is white supremacy—they will meet it all the time whether they like it or not. That is why resistance negotiation is such an important love language; it really is about inviting white progressives to put their politics where their humanity is, to have their politics show up in the emotional by doing this work that has often never been done. Because so often with a progressive politics, people leave their space and go somewhere and do something and then come back. And in that going, there's a certain satisfaction, a certain euphoria, a sense of achievement in the leaving and in the doing. And then there's a certain cushion and safety in coming back. But the reality of systemic change—which is what the whole reckoning is about—is that systems change is about unlearning whiteness, and unlearning whiteness for white progressives is saying that "I'm going to make a different choice when faced with options and the choice I'm going to make is to move somebody else from their place of comfort as I have been moved from my place of comfort."

It's really about saying systems don't work outside of us, systems work through us. Emotional Justice is always about systemic change, but it understands and defines systemic change when it comes to emotionality as the system is maintained through our bodies, our engagement, our relationships—and so we are the dismantlers we've been waiting for. It's about how white progressives who claim a commitment to racial justice engage the work of being the system that shows up to do the dismantling, which means having different conversations, harder ones. Showing up to have those conversations and do that dismantling is doing resistance negotiation and unlearning whiteness in real time. And it might not be every conversation. But the reality has been that there has been practically no conversation, which is why we maintain the voting blocs we maintain. There's really not been that kind of challenge with other white women. We lean back deep into our political comfort of not sharing our political position, who votes differently than we do—but you're actually both being silent—emotionally silent about the work that needs to be done where your body is the system, and the system is working through you. Part of systemic change is about reimagining relationships with white people to unlearn whiteness.

CM: I love the phrasing; it's so evocative and beautiful. In white progressive culture, there's a way in which we are trained to think structurally about race. So we think reading the books and watching the documentaries and maybe donating to XYZ organization is the work, and if we have an emotional connection to racial justice, it's mostly from the position of pitying, feeling sad for—maybe feeling guilty to some extent—say, watching an Ava DuVernay film, feeling the catharsis that I feel bad that this happened to these people—that's mostly our emotional relationship to the whole thing.

It is pity, sadness, confusion versus the emotions coming home to roost between our own friends, between our own family. That kind of emotional engagement is quite rare, and in part I know this because I do it, and I've lost friends. It's very jarring to other people when a white person in a theoretically neutral setting problematizes what's going on, because we do it so rarely. Even in Oakland— and I'm in the progressive of the progressives—and it's still "We're all about racial justice," so we would never question each other's choices or language—because that's really uncouth. You're helping me tap into something. We make fun of the book clubs; there the intellectualization for white people is very compelling. It doesn't ask much of you. You learn about all these systems—and then you feel smarter. And you're still convinced that you have nothing to do with it. Or you have something to do with it, but you're powerless within it. We use that as an excuse for not being personally engaged in your framework of "You are the system"—there is no opting out of it. You are intrinsically a part of it.

EA: Whiteness is framed as always about a superiority. Let's talk about the emotional connection to whiteness, and what that looks like and feels like for you.

CM: I have a paradoxical relationship to whiteness. On the one hand, I know consciously that it benefits me in all these ways that trains me to react emotionally. Another part of me would like to run in the other direction from whiteness, and disassociate from it. I grew up listening to hip hop nonstop, and part of that was because it was awesome, but also part of that was a disassociation with whiteness; dating boys of color as a way of disassociating from whiteness, a lot of trying to be as less-white as I can! Ultimately it doesn't work, it isn't genuine—so trying to unpack the subconscious benefiting from whiteness, and the more on the surface trying to run away from it is interesting for me.

EA: In Emotional Justice, the emotional connection to whiteness is both repulsion and attraction—superiority and insecurity. All of us have to unlearn emotional relationships to whiteness—all of us do, Black, Brown, Indigenous, and white.

CM: To your point about history, I've been thinking a lot about white families' inability to acknowledge the pain and violence within our own family histories. We don't have the emotional muscle to say what's the truth about what's happening in this family. We don't do that within our own families; we're certainly not going to be able to do it on any kind of national level—so I've been thinking a lot about that. So I've been thinking a lot about personal emotional history and emotional national history, and how we're pretty bad at all of it. We have not developed the spiritual muscles that probably if we were doing it more in our emotional and personal lives, we would do it more in our political and national lives.

EA: I would challenge that to say that it is not that there is not the spiritual muscle to tell the truth; it's that the consequences of speaking that truth would be to unravel what whiteness has built. And whiteness has built this very specific world in which it moves to protect itself when it feels in any way threatened. But it has incredible spiritual muscle to manufacture threat where there is none—which is how it treats Black bodies—and to weaponize violence at any hint that whiteness may not be the superior space and state that it has named itself and that it has imposed on the world. But what Emotional Justice is saying is that when it comes to whiteness, part of the challenge is that a narrative is created. There is nothing fragile about whiteness. But there is manufactured threat and manufactured fear—just no fragility. You cannot build a system of supremacy through fragility; you cannot protect it with politics, state violence, and every single weapon that you have from any kind of place of fragility. And so fragility is a manufactured emotion to enable you to not be the dismantler that unraveling and unlearning the language of whiteness would require you to be—

CM: Fragility is a weapon of innocence, of manufacturing this notion of innocence—

EA: Absolutely. And what whiteness does better than anything is weaponize. The emotional connection to whiteness protects itself whenever it feels threatened. And that protection can manifest in multiple ways—it can be a person who is asking challenging questions about the space and the environment in which we live, and why we're making the choices that we make, and it doesn't represent a threat, but because of the whiteness narrative, it's treated as a threat because that's what whiteness has taught everybody. Anything that challenges it must be treated as threat, exterminated, destroyed, and ground into dust. So it's not an absence of spiritual muscle; it's the willingness to marshal everything to protect whiteness.

As we close, going back to your younger self, thinking through what we've talked about. Resistance negotiation—what would you tell your younger self about resistance and whiteness when it comes to engaging your own community of white people and how history has taught you, and how you want to change what living history has taught you about your community?

CM: Honor your outrage; don't honor your superiority, but honor your instincts for wanting to just do things differently than is socially part of your world and your instinct about the wound at the center of whiteness.

EA: And finally, what does unlearning the language of whiteness mean for and to you?

CM: It means moving from a defensive, competitive delusion to be more collective, more joyful, more humble, and hopefully less harmful.

The Emotional Justice Template

Work through your *feelings*: Flee, deny, being defensive, white tears, anger. Wanting to run, being triggered, manufacturing threat, resorting to white tears. Uncertainty, insecurity, frustration, resentment, reward, change.

Reimagine your *focus*: How do I speak the language of whiteness when it comes to being challenged about issues of race and racism? What are the feelings that come up for me?

Build the *future*: Develop and strengthen your discomfort muscles as a crucial element for racial healing, for unlearning, and for decentering whiteness. Resist your instinct to require Black people—particularly Black women—to incentivize you as white people—particularly white women—to stay and do for you what is *your* emotional labor toward racial healing. Resisting this instinct represents decentering whiteness and centering the emotional labor Black, Brown, and Indigenous people often do—and have historically done—to reassure whiteness.

Discussion Points

Using Courtney's example of in-body response—what have been your "flare-ups," and how have you managed, navigated, and engaged when a flare-up has happened?

Describe an incidence of your own defense. Now recount the story using the resistance negotiation model to create a different outcome.

• 6 •

Revolutionary Black Grace

Definition and Action to Be Taken

For Black people globally—in the West, throughout the diaspora, and in Africa—to unlearn the language of whiteness that teaches American blackness as criminal and African blackness as wretched. It is unlearning this single-story exported narrative that dehumanizes and weaponizes global Black people in opposition to one another, sustaining a segregated Blackness that serves whiteness and sustains anti-Blackness. It's about unlearning our identity as part of an emotional economy and replacing it with the Emotional Justice love language of revolutionary Black grace applied to all Black people so that we may love one another more justly and engage our fullest humanity.

Global Black people don't have ordinary trauma. So we can't have ordinary grace. We require a grace that is specific to and for us, and that recognizes our lived experience of centuries-deep injustice and harm, of movement building and resistance. We need the kind of grace that recognizes our work of revolution. It is because of those three things—lived experience, centuries of harm, and resistance via movement building—that this Emotional Justice love language for global Black people is a grace that is Black and revolutionary.

Breakdown

Revolutionary Black grace is about building emotional connections among global Black people to one another's Blackness—in America, across the diaspora, and in Africa. We global Black people have created ways to survive the unsurvivable, so we can—indeed we must—make a way to invest in healing among one another. It starts by identifying how global Black people speak the language of whiteness.

Global Black people were nurtured via narratives of whiteness that made American Blackness immoral and wicked, and African Blackness pitiful and inferior. That nurturing created a repulsion toward one another. It made our identity an emotional economy of internalized self-hate that stifles our healing, and only feeds a narrative of Blackness as inferior.

Revolutionary Black grace invites us to engage one another centering a love we may not yet have, a belonging we may not yet feel, and a brotherhood, a sisterhood beyond ideas and ideology. It requires that we reimagine our Blackness in our own image—a panorama of browns due to a journey and a history that forever changed us. That means approaching one another as global Black people with more care, tenderness, and compassion.

This is about Black intimacies, Black humanity, and navigating turbulent terrain of history, rupture, trauma, betrayal, and new beginnings. It is about replacing an emotional economy that was about division and separation that served whiteness, and developing, strengthening, and sustaining a Blackness that honors the totality, geography, and specificity of our historical journeys from Africa to America, Europe, the Caribbean, and Brazil to survive brutal systems.

Revolutionary Black grace is a love language for and toward global Black people about melanin wrapped in unfamiliar tenderness.

Global Black People and the Language of Whiteness

Global Black people speak the language of whiteness via a narrative that taught us what our Blackness meant and how it came to be, and therefore shaped how we saw ourselves, one another, and, especially important, how we didn't want to be seen.

This narrative reduced kingdoms and culture to savage nothingness, fit only to be molded by melanin-free hands and then kept in service to melanin-free worlds. The narrative taught a notion of Africa, the cradle of the universe and the origin of humanity, renaming it the "Dark Continent," as a place with a savage, brooding, predatory people who were tree swingers, people eaters, and hut dwellers, a continent permanently on its knees, arms outstretched, with distended bellies, poverty stricken, war torn, begging to be saved again and again by the West—read white people.

That was the single story of Africa. It was a teaching that shaped a relationship to and an understanding of Africa that fed shame, poverty porn, and an urgent desire to have no part of this land or the people who came from it.

That single story traveled, even if global Black people didn't. It landed in playgrounds, classrooms, workplaces, kitchens, and hallways all over the world, taking shape in souls and minds, and manifesting in hands pointing at African folk, pitying them, or laughing, disparaging, teasing, hurting again and again.

This single story was not a one-way ticket. Parallel narratives of African Americans as thugs and gangstas, irresponsible, criminal, and lazy were fed to those in Africa, and to the world. Those narratives had passports, even though we didn't. They traveled and settled into bellies and bodies that shaped how Africans saw Black folk in America and, equally important, how Africans didn't want to be seen.

These narratives about an African Blackness and an American Blackness create a Blackness that centers whiteness. It is one that nurtures a segregated Blackness. It is anti-Blackness. It is an emotional economy of division and separation fed by feelings about Blackness that reimagine your roots as rubbish to be discarded, not claimed. This is how the emotional economy worked—our value appreciated the more we despised one another's Blackness.

The language of whiteness despises pan-Africanism, because it is a philosophy that connects, celebrates, and honors our Blackness. And this language does not nurture connection among global Black people; it is hungry for a separated Blackness. Pan-Africanism ends isolation and fosters connection. Connection builds global community. Global community strengthens fiscal economies, elevates an opportunity to practice revolutionary Black grace—and kills the emotional economy. However, from the perspective of Emotional Justice, the philosophy of pan-Africanism does not mean that the emotional connection to Blackness shaped by whiteness is healed—that requires emotional work. That is emotional labor global Black people need to do.

Global Black folks across the diaspora are fluent in racist bullshit; it is our Black mother tongue. We have been raised in a language of systems, of stories about who we are and how we came to be. That narrative is spoken by industries—the worlds of politics, education, media, beauty, art, and entertainment—and it has consequences. It teaches us to speak internal languages of doubt, insecurity, and absence of value, that Blackness is about deficit and whiteness about world building and people saving. That is the language of reimagining history to serve injustice, entrench inequity, and feed white supremacy. This is the politics of whiteness; millions of global Black folk get this. That they get this politically doesn't always mean they get it emotionally, and it is in the emotional that harm is perpetuated and that revolutionary Black grace—approaching one another with empathy—matters.

You're the Problem! No, You Are!

We as global Black people practice anti-Blackness through our notions about and our name-calling of one another.

Africa had dual narratives of the guaranteed prosperity on America's streets and the problem of the Black American on those same streets. Because of this, African Americans were to be avoided at all costs. And that narrative manifested in the bodies of Africans who would swerve, dip, and dive to avoid African Americans—and tell them so, literally tell African Americans that their success as Africans could not be guaranteed if they as Africans were, or stayed, around them.

A part of the narrative was blaming Black Americans for what was judged as their failure to adequately flourish in this America of prosperity and opportunity. Too many Africans would mischaracterize institutional racism as individual failings. It's a dangerous lie, a particularly jarring and incendiary narrative. It triggers deep historical wounds, and it performs the particular work of white supremacy and anti-Blackness. It is the emotional economy at work, weaponizing narrative to divide Blackness, blame Blackness, all while centering whiteness and preserving an accountability-free whiteness.

America's narratives about Africa manifest in how Black folk in America hurt, tease, disregard, and disrespect Africans who ended up in America. The shade of their skin would be disparaged, their accents laughed at; hurtful names would be hurled in playgrounds and homerooms.

What Did You Call Me?

Weaponized narratives show up in language, name-calling, and descriptions designed to wound and draw blood. Kenyan-born filmmaker Peres Owino's documentary *Bound: Africans vs African-Americans*, about two brothers separated by history and fighting to find their way back to each other, features contributors who demonstrate that. In the documentary's town hall, global Black people share what they heard, what was said, and what they were told about one another.

Here's what some African American contributors shared:

> "I've heard about a word that some West Africans use in reference to African Americans. It's *akata*—I looked it up, it's a Yoruba word, it means 'wild animal.'"

> "I was having a conversation with an African man who asked me: Why do African American women wear headwraps, when we're not African?"

> "Some of the Africans in Sierra Leone were calling me 'pumage'—do you know what *pumage* means? 'White boy.'"

Here's what some African contributors shared:

"You can actually see African Americans—when they were on African soil—treat Africans in a way that they feel themselves as separate, and they're accepting the stereotypes of white people—the way they look at Africans."

"I had an African American friend who called me 'spear-chucker.'"

"I came to this country [the USA] from Cote d'Ivoire, Ivory Coast. I was ten years old. And I was dropped in Harlem in the early '90s. Next thing I know I'm being bullied for being African. I don't even know where they got 'African booty scratcher' from."

"Before coming to America, I was told stay away from African Americans—they're so violent, they're so dangerous. So I had that notion that I shouldn't be involved with them, because I'd end up in trouble and be shipped back to Africa."

"African Americans don't take advantage of the opportunity here. They're lazy; they're not serious."

I have lived and worked in New York and Ghana. I have heard versions of these sorts of comments from both Ghanaians and from African Americans. These are colliding traumas from historical wounds of oppressive systems. This is the emotional economy at work, sowing division, sustaining separation. The single aim is to ensure that we wouldn't look at and into one another and recognize family. Instead we would see someone we loathe, someone we would never want to be —someone who isn't like us, doesn't understand us, and isn't part of us. In all of these ways, global Black people speak the language of whiteness.

Let's Define and Find Power in Our Global Blackness

Being Black in America, being Black from Africa in America, being Black in Britain or a nation in Europe, being Black in Africa—each is a distinct experience. The language of whiteness has shaped our particular Blackness in each of the places where we are born, raised, and schooled, where we love and work. Just because the language of whiteness has a hand in this shaping should not mean that we don't work to heal what it tried to break, and build what it tried to destroy—in other words, we need to work to reestablish our severed connection to one another, but on our own terms, centering our own lens.

To be born and raised in America is to carry a Blackness shaped by the journey of enslavement. The loss of land, freedom, culture, language, and heritage created a Blackness of beginnings, severed lineage, and a remaking in order to survive. "Loss remakes you. I was black and a history of terror had produced that identity," writes Saidiya Hartman in *Lose Your Mother: A Journey along the Atlantic Slave Route*. That remaking holds a deep legacy of untreated trauma, but it also carries power and purpose. It means creating culture; remaking yourself; finding beauty in your bones, your Blackness; and actively, collectively resisting a narrative that named you nothing.

To be born and raised in Britain is to carry a Blackness shaped by colonialism. Britain was then the Motherland. This Blackness was about diminishing rituals and histories. Your language remained; your sense of self was changed. To be thought of and seen as British was an aspiration—*the* aspiration. It meant that your Blackness was reduced, that you centered whiteness in order to achieve, to become successful. This racism came with perfect manners from a violence wrapped in cut-glass accents, starched white shirts, crisp collars, and tea in china cups. There was also enslavement by the British. And there was the way Blackness made Britishness something uniquely theirs, with resistance movements that demanded a humanity from a whiteness that dehumanized. Blackness shaped Britain, creating culture through food, resistance, and music that told the story of this journey from grime to traditions that would seep into and remain part of Britain's cultural landscape.

To be born and raised in Ghana is to carry a Blackness shaped both by the power of African ancestry, culture, ritual, and belonging, and by the pain of colonialism and the wound from severed families due to enslavement. Colonialism was about British whiteness as superior and African darkness as inferior. Your ancestral traditions and rituals, your religion—all carried such depth and power, but were ridiculed and rubbished, replaced by a Christianity with a brown-haired, white-skinned savior who schoolchildren were taught to bow down to, to pray to, to worship. Whiteness was worship. Colonialism created a particular inferiority, whose legacy lingers and manifests in economies that privilege what is not homegrown or homemade but is instead manufactured on other soils; and the mere fact of its being imported—and therefore not African—rendered it superior. Enslavement robbed families of loved ones, creating a forever-changed nation, and lingering wounds that are too often overlooked.

It is crucial for global Black people to know and honor that there are two wounds from enslavement that require healing: that of the kidnapped person and what they endure, and that of the family and nation forever scarred by this loss. That's how the trauma shaped Blackness in Ghana. And it is a trauma unspoken when it comes to repair—and specifically the work of reparations. Enslavement scarred Africa as well as the nations to which all those enslaved would be taken. Both wounds matter. So a reparative approach honors the particular journey in America, Britain, and the Caribbean, but frames that repair in connection with and relationship to Africa. That too is a practice of revolutionary Black grace and an unlearning of whiteness.

In America, Britain, and Ghana, Black folk had to survive the common language of violence and brutality. In all three places, there was loss. Loss is a common language among us as global Black people. But it has different dialects.

Loss, Trauma, and Comparisons

Loss is an intimate part of global Blackness. Britain was an empire. America became a superpower. Africa had kingdoms. All global Black people lost something through systems of oppression where the language of whiteness ruled under brutal lash, stolen native tongues, and charred skin.

Unfortunately, the issue is that global Black people compare and judge our losses. We tell one another that our loss is way worse than yours. We reach into the wounds of historical untreated trauma, wrap our pain around our mother tongue, fashion an insult, and target it at a man or a woman or child who looks just like us, or a shade of us. We are prosecutors, presenting damning evidence of deficit, intending to diminish and destroy. Devastatingly, we succeed.

Africans tell African Americans, "What do you know of our trauma? You're not African. You're American. Why must you always say racism, racism, racism?" African Americans tell Africans in the US, "You're here! In America! You're Black! Speak English. This ain't Africa! You're taking our jobs; you think you're better than us." And back and forth, and back and forth we go. We wound, retreat, and reemerge with fresh insults and unfresh trauma. Such is a lingering legacy of combined anti-Blackness and the language of whiteness.

This is a weaponizing of emotions—feelings of belonging, betrayal, and broken brotherhood—wielded like deadly samurai swords. This weaponizing entrenches historical separation and cultural segregation. What does that look like? Award-winning filmmaker dream hampton's documentary *Let's Get Free: The Black August Hip Hop Project* shows us.

The film is in tribute to incarcerated political prisoners. It focuses on social justice and Black liberation, and features African American hip hop artists performing in New York, Cuba, and South Africa. On their South African leg, the artists attended the 2001 World Racism Conference in Durban, South Africa. There was an exchange between African Americans and Black South Africans that reveals this legacy of losses and comparisons.

The hip hop artists sit on a panel behind a desk with mics looking out over an audience that includes young Black South Africans, and international media. The artists share messages of oppression, trauma, and loss stemming from being Black in America. Sections of the Black South African audience, arms folded, faces set, stare at them as they speak.

An African American woman, wearing a bright-yellow windbreaker, mic gripped, addresses the audience: "Coming to Africa, we are African Americans—and we don't know the African experience. Apartheid in South Africa—it is 90 percent Black; it's not comparable to the many abuses that we experience in the United States, which is still a majority white country."

Some of the young Black South Africans roll their eyes. They are becoming agitated. The exchange continues.

Another hip hop artist in shades and a black beanie says, "Us as kidnapped Africans in America, we fully understand our role in Africans' liberation worldwide."

After several more statements about oppression and racism in America from the panel and the international media, the Black South Africans grow even more agitated. The mic is finally passed to a Black South African high school student. Hand raised, with pushed-back natural hair and a white T-shirt with a map of South Africa around her neck, she starts to speak. She is angry. She stares directly at each of the artists, and sweeps her arm to indicate that her comments are to all the hip hop artists on the panel: "For next time—or any other time—you come, *we're here*! And we deserve to be *heard*! The past injustices that happened to us are *still* happening to us and are still going on! It may seem that under the banner of this conference everything is fine! Everything is not so well! I am a student—I still suffer to go to school. My parents still need to struggle! How far can *you* empathize with *us*? *never*. Because what *we* feel, *you* don't feel."

She hands the mic over, turns her back, turns back around, and crosses her arms facing the artists, face stony. Spotty applause breaks out; it comes from other Black South Africans.

Uneasiness, hurt, anger, and contempt move between the South Africans in the audience toward the African Americans on the panel. The air changes. Violence hovers. Stares are lengthening between panelists and audience members. Murmuring in South African languages grows, choking, accusing. The artists shift in their bodies; they exchange glances, the kind that say, "Shit's about to go down."

One of the hip hop artists responds, gesturing constantly with his hands, his voice emotional, passionate: "Listen! I understand what you're sayin' 'bout tryna empathize or whateva!

But at least *you* guys still had *your* language! *we* don't even know who *we* are! Imagine if you didn't even know who you are? Imagine! *you* know who *you* are—who's your mother, who's your grandfather, who's your grandmother! So you have some sense of who you are! We don't even know who we are!"

In this exchange, shared trauma becomes a litigated history of loss versus loss, of mine is worse than yours, of what do you know about what it is to be my kind of Black. In this case, this emotional litigation is between South Africans and African Americans.

In the documentary, the exchange doesn't end in a peaceful coming together. There is a drifting apart between the two groups, but the unease, the hurt words, the resentment remain.

This chasm that divides us as global Black people is a supremacy of Black traumas and unheard hurt. Prosecuting loss buries already buried trauma even deeper into global Black bodies—it becomes a coffin that buries us all.

This pain becomes accusation and moves from the personal to the political, from the individual to the institutional. It then travels into our movements that philosophize about a pan-Africanism but don't recognize how untreated traumas feed an emotional relationship to our Blackness, not an ideological or philosophical one. What that means is that the division, the misunderstanding, the hurt, the anger, the resentment emerge to influence how we work, lead, and build with one another. It becomes a back-and-forth about who belongs where and who doesn't, what is owed and to whom, and on and on and on. What it does, fundamentally, is divide, and entrench division. It causes us to implode; it causes our movements to implode.

Scars from the Language of Whiteness

These scars are not only between Black folk in America and Africa. A segregated Blackness narrative dominates across parts of Africa too. During my first trip to South Africa, I remember the open hostility, dismissal, and judgment from Black South Africans toward me. I was judged as an African who wasn't specifically South African. This too has a term, *amankwerekwere*, meaning "people from Africa." Sounds strange, right? Especially since I was from Africa, just as they were. The language of whiteness flourished in South Africa too, creating an Africa that was wretched, corrupt, and criminal, and specifically separating South Africa from this "other Africa." That is why unlearning the language of whiteness is for all of us—global Black folks too. South African writer Sisonke Msimang writes about this in her visionary memoir *Always Another Country*.

From Southern Africa to West Africa. In Senegal, a friend shares a story of an incident in Dakar, where a man told her that her Blackness is not his. They have a name for those like her: *nnack*—when you hear it said, it sounds like someone hawking up phlegm from their throat, ready to spit—it feels as it sounds.

Pause. Breathe. Close your eyes. It is here we so need revolutionary Black grace. What cannot win in our fight for full liberation is a divided, segregated Blackness. We are global Black family. We cannot heal with one another like this. We simply cannot.

Between Us ... Black Women and Men

It is between us as Black women and men that these scars show up as generational inheritance. They are wounds soaked in blood, bone, burden, and brutality. Revolutionary Black grace between us is tender territory that must be carefully navigated. For Black women, there is—and has been—an emotional labor engaged in for Black men that is historical, transformative, and traumatic. That labor is how we love one another; it is how we hurt one another—it cannot be how we heal one another. Emotional Justice requires emotional labor—from all of us. Our freedom movements were the result of the efforts of women and men; that is our history. The erasure train has traveled from Africa to America across continents, cities, and communities, removing Black women from seats at tables of resistance, disappearing our stories, reducing our sacrifice, and diminishing our struggle. Erasure is the language of trauma; it feeds the emotional economy. It does nothing for our healing. Doing this emotional labor is not a question about whether or not we love one another as Black people; it is about how we love one another, and how that love must reimagine emotional labor as part of our collective healing process.

We did not get free alone, we do not survive alone, we cannot heal alone—we thrive together. That togetherness requires a revolutionary Black grace in which emotional labor is recognized, respected, and equally divided. There can be no Emotional Justice among us as global Black people without the equal division of emotional labor.

Honoring Our Journey, Finding Our Connection

We can recognize distinct Black experience without creating Black supremacies. We can honor the specificity and the distinction of a Blackness shaped by America, shaped by Africa and the Caribbean, and shaped by Europe—and how that Blackness shows up in Britain, in France, and in Africa. Each matters. We must recognize how historical oppressive systems had an expansive hand in reimagining our Blackness.

In other words, we can honor our unique and specific Blackness, but frame it in connection with a global Blackness. That globality goes back to Africa, a continent of beginnings and of remakings, but also one of an enduring land, with myriad stories. Our road to healing as global Black people honors, revels in, and acknowledges—it doesn't diminish. That is how global Black people unlearn the language of whiteness, develop emotional connections to one another, and replace the emotional economy with revolutionary Black grace.

Global Black people fought for our freedom across Africa, in America, across Europe. We inspired one another. The independence movement of Ghana in the 1950s and 1960s parallels the rise of the civil rights movement in America. In the UK, there were freedom and resistance movements rising up to fight oppression. Courage was all of ours. Leaders such as Kwame Nkrumah, Ghana's first post-Independence Black president, and the Ghanaian women who funded the independence movement; Winnie Mandela of South Africa; Malcolm X; and Martin Luther King Jr. were all moved and shaped by a global Blackness. Martin Luther King Jr. came to Nkrumah's inauguration and spoke of the connection between Blackness in America and what was happening in Ghana, as did Fannie Lou Hamer when she went to Senegal. All of it speaks to the freedoms we fought for and the systems we navigated to survive.

Because of these journeys, revolutionary Black grace honors a Blackness that, yes, has been commodified, criminalized, demonized, deified, desired—but one we must make our own without diminishing one another. This is careful, challenging work. It is a path that covers millions of miles. And it is a practice of healing that evicts a centering of whiteness.

Our Blackness is interconnected, evolving and changing, while the language of whiteness stays the same and has the same objective. This language always seeks to bury your youness and create a striving to be more somebody else. In being somebody else, you step away from an interconnected Blackness. No healing, no grace, no freedom comes from that.

Black Privilege Is Not the Answer

The contemporary story of Blackness centers America. That centering has consequences. It leads to a privileging of your Blackness, not connecting it to that of other Black folk in other parts of the world. There is a parallel narrative in places such as the UK, the "You have it better than the Blacks in the USA" narrative. This is a nurtured story, a fiction designed to hold up your Britishness with an exhale of "Thank God we're not them." It's a deadly lie.

We cannot get to healing by walking a path of privilege. We cannot replace white privilege with African privilege or African American privilege and expect to clearly hear one another as Africans and Black peoples of African descent around the world. Refusing to adopt privilege doesn't mean that our healing journeys don't include colliding traumas and conflict. They do. They will. There is centuries' worth of untreated trauma to unpack and heal. But we can't do that as we have been.

Revolutionary Black grace makes space to shape the conversation, honor the foundation, recognize the tradition, and reimagine our union. That starts by rebuking as lies these narratives of deficit and notions of supremacy—white and Black.

The Emotional, Not the Political

This work is about our emotional connection to our Blackness and to the Blackness of one another. An emotional connection to Blackness is not the same as a political one. Blackness is absolutely personal and political—that is a centuries-long marriage. That's not what I mean.

You can be philosophically pan-African, but your emotional connection to Blackness is not necessarily about those politics—a politics of possibility and connectivity that unifies Black people from around the world and centers global Blackness. That is a neat, clear philosophy. But your emotionality is not neat; it is messy—how can it not be, given the history and its legacy of untreated trauma? Your emotional connection may have been nurtured by deficiency; by how you've been loved; by how you've not been loved; by how you've been hurt; by how you've been treated, rejected, and discriminated against and how you have witnessed that toward family—that, too, is a generational inheritance. All these things shape your sense of self. So you may politically understand, but emotionally respond. That is emotionality masquerading as ideology. And it can fuck shit up. It does. And it has.

We see this in movements whose political ideology aligns, but that still implode. The reparations movement in the US highlights this phenomenon. There are multiple intersecting issues that we mischaracterize as political, when they are in fact about the emotional. One of those issues is an ongoing fight to disconnect an American blackness from a global Blackness. That hurts the healing of us as a global Black people. Those advocating that disconnect use tactics of attack, lambasting, and vicious critique—all weapons of whiteness and, increasingly, wokeness—but also adopted within global Blackness, designed to entrench division. If our aim is to repair what has been broken, lost, and stolen, but our approach is to separate one Blackness from another, then we are engaging the weapons of whiteness while claiming that this is healing. That shit doesn't work. Not for healing.

There is a trauma among us that goes beyond language. There are connections among us that break down beyond legacy. What also lies between us as global Black people—across North America, in Europe, and in Africa—is a range of emotions: betrayal, resentment, a yearning, an anger, a sadness, a mourning, a magic, a beauty, a belonging, a desire for belonging, the pain of rupture. There is all of this between all of us.

History stripped millions of an identity, but not of a cultural memory. The DNA of the drum creates a global Black drumline, and in it we can find one another, and honor one another's journey. That is revolutionary Black grace.

The badassness of Blackness is universally understood, from culture, to art, to fashion, to food, to emulated beauty. We are swagger and flava, and all the things. What still connects us is Africa. Our first home. That doesn't mean we as global Black people all feel connected to Africa. We may not. We do not.

Our Blackness may be connected to our roots in the Southern states or to the history of Chicago or Detroit. It may flex its cultural muscles to soundtracks of London or Nottingham or Birmingham. All of these are part of our Blackness; all must be acknowledged. So this is not about the denial of the geographical spaces and places that shaped you, that you call home.

Home sits uneasy on tongues trained by the West's particular love language of violence toward Black bodies. America is a superpower—one that understands itself in superlatives: first this, biggest that, big, bigger, biggest, biggerlicious. To be Black in America is to be the descendant of those who built it, and to be simultaneously rejected by it. This does not mean that Black folks in America are not American, or that

America is not their home. Absolutely not. They are, and it is. It simply means there is an uneasiness in this relationship to this history within this nation. Poet Hafiyah Geter reminds us that this is "a nation that doesn't love someone who looks like me." America's better self is rooted in Blackness, resistance, movement building, and a refusal to capitulate to the whiteness narrative of beasts and burdens.

Britain was an empire. It's relationship of superiority wreaked havoc with Black and Brown people. That superiority was a delusion. It manifests in two ways: a constant erasure of Britain's violence in her former colonies, and a romanticizing of that time as one of a manufactured greatness. This doesn't mean that Black folks in Britain don't love where they live, haven't built homes and family and community. They absolutely do and have. So much of Europe's wealth and Britain's power is rooted in Blackness from the Caribbean and Africa.

Finding home within one another means staying when it gets hard and when your soul connects to conflict, not comfort. But making a home takes time and action. It means engaging in an ongoing practice of empathy toward those who look like you—even when they don't feel you, and you don't feel them. Revolutionary Black grace means finding homes in and with one another by going on journeys of decentering whiteness and of honoring the full expanse of our Blackness across regions, countries, and continents. Doing that is a practice, not just a philosophy.

An Exchange with
Tulaine Montgomery and Nguhi Mwaura

I am talking here with Tulaine Montgomery, an African American and co-CEO of New Profit; and Nguhi Mwaura, a Kenyan and host of Rethinking Possible, a global podcast focusing on innovators finding solutions to big issues. Both have traveled between the US and Africa.

Tulaine Montgomery is **TM**. Nguhi Mwaura is **NM**. Esther Armah is **EA**.

EA: The language of whiteness segregates Blackness; we then perpetuate it with a my-kind-of-Black approach and attitude. What does that phrase "your kind of Black" mean to you? How does that manifest in the way you move?

TM: I struggle with that even as a notion. I was raised as a child of the diaspora. My father is an ethnomusicologist, a master drummer, named by the ancient tradition of a village in Ghana many years ago when he was a young man. He came up spending many years of his life in Mali, Cuba, and many other places understanding the power of percussion, culture, economy, and identity. That's who raised me. Because of that, there's a way that I never really settled well with the notion of "division." In some ways I had an almost naïve view of how easy it should be for Black-race-identified people to get along, to see each other, to lift each other up.

NM: I grew up on the African continent. I have only known myself to be part of the majority, and so Blackness was not an identity I took on until I was navigating situations where people were majority white. Black was for African Americans; it wasn't for Africans, because everyone is Black. I've only reckoned with my Blackness as an adult, and it has meant different things at different stages. It's been an ever-evolving journey, and there's still a lot I need to grow and integrate.

EA: Can you talk a bit more about learning that Blackness was for African Americans, and so in some ways there was an element of Blackness that did not include you?

NM: Growing up, my parents were the second generation born after Independence. They were born right at Independence, so they've never known a British overlord per se, but they have known people who aspired to Britishness—and essentially, it's whiteness. And that's the pathway that was carved for success. You needed access to white spaces; you needed to be able to speak English in a certain way. You needed to go to school with other white kids, and that was your way to success. When the choice was learning Latin or learning ki-swahili at school, we'd go with learning Latin, because that's going to take you further than speaking ki-swahili. And so it was only in high school I started to ask: Why is that? There had always been in my upbringing a kind of inferiority that had been embedded around Africanness, and African things were seen as backward. My access into Blackness has a lot of times been through African American thought leaders, media. I see it like an opaque curtain that we look at each other through, and that curtain is often whiteness. And so African Americans are receiving messages about what Africa is, what it represents, and how backward and full of war. And we were receiving messages about who African Americans were through their media. And so African Americans are in the ghetto, they're in jail, and they don't work hard. And we cannot see each other clearly through this curtain.

EA: You're Kenyan, Nguhi, and I remember Kenya was the model for racial healing that Archbishop Desmond Tutu invoked when I went to South Africa to learn about their racial healing model of Truth and Reconciliation. It's in-

teresting because listening to you is a reminder that being on the African continent doesn't mean you escape the
language of whiteness. The colonization took its toll and
shaped our Africanness in ways that harm our humanity
and shape our nations with a legacy that's still here today.
Let's talk about expanding our idea of Blackness incorporating all the journeys we have taken as a people. We are
taught about each other without knowing each other. I
was born in London. I knew about America, having never
stepped foot in America. Some of what I learned was on
TV, sitcoms about Black family life. Some of what I knew
had nothing to do with Black people and how Black people
were actually living. So, in that sense, this is the language
of whiteness at work—this narrative of how the world is,
and who you are in that world. Talk about how the lens of
whiteness has shaped Blackness.

TM: For many years, I paid a lot of gratitude to my family and
a lot of pride in that upbringing I described earlier—the
fact that my father would come home from Mali and show
me videos of Malian women, and he would say "Tulaine,
look at her feet—those look like your feet." Something as
simple as that embedded something in me. And so I was
really proud for a long time about the fact that I knew
stories told to me as an American about the continent of
Africa were lies. I came in knowing I expect you to lie to
me. To some degree, the more elite the institution feed-
ing me the information, the more acute I anticipate the lie
to be. What I've come to understand recently is that the
resistance I was raised in was a response, and a reaction to
whiteness. And so, for me, a stage for growth and healing
is: How can I actually experience my life and make choices
that are not a reaction or a fight against whiteness? And

that honestly feels like a whole new terrain, because I've come up so steeped in the rejection of and resistance to the lies white supremacy would tell me about Black people.

NM: That is so powerful! If all that brings us together is resistance and resistance to white supremacy, then what do we have? I follow on Instagram Dr. Yaba Blay—she has all these memes, and what she does is find ways to tie Blackness across different contexts, so it's not just one type—it will include African Americans, Africans, and whenever there's a glimpse of things we share across cultures, things that have persisted—it gives me so much joy. It helps me know that we are tied together by more than what whiteness has told the other, and those are the moments that I live for, those are the moments that affirm that it isn't just about resistance—even though so much of the identity of taking it on has been about resistance. When there are those moments—like Tulaine you were saying with the feet—there's things that connect us to the mitochondrial DNA of that first ancestor—those are the moments that give me the most joy in Blackness.

EA: Part of what a revolutionary Black grace is doing and saying is we can build the Blackness that we want and we say what it is, and having said that, we can then engage and exchange from that place—thoughts?

TM: We global Black people have to get more bold at discerning when we're being lied to about one another. We're so willing to believe all that we've been told—all the failings, the shortcomings, the inconsistencies, and we're so unwilling to see, never mind lift up, the genius, the resilience, the creativity, the joy—it's so hard. One of the hardest moments I had when I was in Boston around these issues was with a friend, Haitian American, who loved all things

French, and yet had a whole set of stories about Black Americans—excluding me, saw me as "an exception"—who she interacted with. I said to my friend, "Why is it that I can see and have love and reverence to not only the legacy of Toussaint but the genius that is happening right now in Haiti, and the stuff about failed economy isn't my primary story about Haiti, but you're here, in the United States, and unwilling to see that there is brilliance and beauty here?"

NM: The wound and the loss that I feel, particularly as an African, is that of just being ignored. Africa is never seen as a place that has a future, that has anything interesting going on, and the narratives are so simplified. We're not allowed our full humanity. And I do believe that has an impact on global Black people, because where you tie back to—and if you believe those things about that place—then inevitably you believe those things about you.

EA: What do we have to unlearn about ourselves, each other, and how we engage as global Black people? Revolutionary Black grace is not about an ideal of love. It's about a practice that is unfamiliar; it is starting with "I am going to unlearn the instinct to decide who you are, before I know who you are."

NM: It's something I think about almost daily because I find myself often betraying my ideals for capitalism, because I need to make a living. Those are the moments in which I find myself seeing how white supremacy is at work, and then figuring out how I make it work for myself. But what that leaves on the table is: What am I allowing to continue by being part of these systems? And it's something that I think about every day because none of us is bigger than the entire system. It begins in actually seeing that white supremacy. For me that starts with my childhood. And I don't think my parents were trying to induct me into white supremacy—but that's what they did. They were the facilitators of telling me, this is what success looks like, and success very often looks white, and this is what we aspire to for you. And so having to unlearn that—the idea of Africa not being global—it's insane. I read this book and for the first time I saw myself, and my identity as an African—and I was eighteen! And I went and studied African Studies in the US, and the absurdity of that—because that's what I was primed for, that you go to the West because that's "global"—that's what counts. I didn't end up going, and I stayed in Africa, and I'm so grateful because that's where my unlearning began.

EA: Let's talk betrayal and belonging—where have you felt it, where have you done it, and why?

NM: In my complicity of betraying African Americans in the white spaces I occupied. There was so much tolerance for me because I was African, not African American, especially from white people. There was almost this festishization, but also this infantilization of me. It wasn't quite the same with African Americans. With them there was this fear and animosity. So I found myself trying to navigate those spaces with a lot more freedom to say truths. I also thought: *How am I playing into their narrative of who they think I am as an African, and the truths I will not say because I am not African American, and because I don't have that same experience?* My ancestors were not enslaved people—what are they willing to hear from me, that they are not willing to hear from an African American? I need to decide what I'm here to do. I'm in this space—the philanthropy space—for this amount of time; what am I no longer willing to betray? I cannot continue to play into this narrative the way that it has been playing out.

EA: What does revolutionary Black grace mean to you and for global Black people? Let's close with that. For me it means we don't all have the same relationship to our Blackness, and we don't all have to, to find ways to move together.

NM: Revolutionary black grace comes in moving beyond the magical. We are still here, and we are here to be known, and to know each other in our fullness and in our flawedness. Beyond grace is the idea of: Can I see you, can I understand you? Am I interested in your experience, and in being as reciprocal as we can be? Can we find the moments where we resonate more than the moments where we diverge?

The Emotional Justice Template

Work through your *feelings*: Hurt, anger, feeling unheard, joy, power, finding community

Reimagine your *focus*: Where have you seen the language of whiteness spoken by global Black people? How have you, or those within your environment, engaged that language?

Build the *future*: Center compassion, empathy, and an approach that says, "Let me not decide who you are before I know who you are" toward all Black people as a practice that begins to honor the totality of Blackness and ends a segregated Blackness.

Discussion Points

Nguhi highlights the work of Dr. Yaba Blay, who uses her Instagram to show all the ways global Black people are connected—check out her IG@professionalblackgirl and choose two posts that demonstrate this. Share with your circle and discuss the connections you see, how they make you feel, and where you see yourself in those connections.

Explore and define what revolutionary Black grace might look like for you, and within your community.

Become the Change You Claim

Breathe. So here we are. Journeying through the pages of this book, you explored this Emotional Justice roadmap, the love languages, and the unlearning.

This is all of our work to do—white, Black, Brown, Indigenous. The chapters reveal that our work is not the same. So you begin by asking, Where do I start?

You start where you are with what you have where you work, live, learn, and love. This is about building from a "right now, right where I am" space. This is not magic. It is the process of developing a practice, a racial healing practice of Emotional Justice.

Your trusty tool is the Emotional Justice template, and its three steps:

1. Work through your **feelings**
2. Reimagine your **focus**
3. Build the **future**

Emotional Justice is about community. You build one by first doing the work, and in doing the work, connection begins.

That first connection is to parts of yourself that are unexplored, that feel uncomfortable, and where there is resistance. That's the first *feeling* step we must all take and work through. Connection is not performance; it is action and accountability. It is developing your racial healing practice.

The Emotional Justice template is now your constant companion and guide as you step away from the pages and into your places of labor, learning, and loving. Your feelings might be all over the place; your focus too. That's OK. It's a lot. So let's carve out a beginning for each of us, for all of us. Carry the template with you. It's not so much a comfort or shield, but it offers a context.

Remember, doing your emotional work is not a one-and-done exercise. You'll move between the parts of your world— your community, your place of work, your place of learning. You are not alone, but you may feel lonely at times. You will start and stop. You will come back to this work as you move through your world—that's fine; practice happens that way. But return you must, we must. Know that it's not a stroll but a sustained marathon of a power walk.

We cannot assign our racial healing to begin, emerge, and be done in a quarter 1 fiscal-year timeline. We would like to—we have often treated racial healing that way. But it is not how we speak Emotional Justice love languages.

This requires a long-game focus and ongoing engagement and commitment. What we have is a roadmap, ourselves, and one another. We have what we need. Let's journey together.

Your Emotional Justice racial healing practice begins now.

Discussion Guide

This short discussion guide uses the Emotional Justice template of *work through your feelings, reimagine your focus, and build the future* and is designed to open up space for you to have, hold, and stay through an Emotional Justice–focused discussion.

Work through your feelings

Talk about the feelings that emerged as you read the chapters of the book.

Reimagine your focus

Share examples and stories of how you have seen and experienced the language of whiteness spoken across sectors, in organizations within your own experience, in those within your circle, and by colleagues outside your circle.

Build the future

Share a scenario or situation centering whiteness from your own experience or within your organization; now retell the story decentering whiteness. Share how the change would transform the space you are in—whether that is labor, learning, or leisure space.

Acknowledgments

Writing this book has been a journey of dreaming, being rejected, deep insecurity, having nightmares, and back again. I stopped writing it because I didn't think I could. I stopped because I no longer knew what I wanted say. I stopped because I became scared to say it. And then I started again. And again. And again. Affirmed by dear, dear chosen family who cheered me on, called me out, reminded me of how far I had come, and celebrated with me along the way.

Gratitude. Appreciation. Familyhood. I am loved and shaped by women and men across the global spaces I call home. Ma and Pa, your journeys are extraordinary; they created an adventurer in me. Thank you to my sisters and brother, Liza, Charlotte, Hilda, and John. My chosen family spans three continents, and they love me to life. In the UK, Francesca Adedeji, Joy Francis, Philomena Francis, and Debbie Robinson are the most precious of sisters—you are so loved. In the US, Beverley Prentice-Thomas, Randy Thomas, Joan Morgan, Mama Morgan, and Greg Morgan—you are home. My Pleasure Ninja sistren Brittney Cooper, Treva B. Lindsey, and Kaila Adia-Story are the baddest of badass Black chicks who are now dear friends. My LA Black Brit fam Christabel Nsiah-Buadi and Joanne Griffith-Poplar—we've all walked in and worked through the wahala of journalism, and sustained our beautiful sisterhood. In Ghana, Efam Dovi, Madonna Kendona, Taaka Awori, Ruby Ofori, and my Naija sistren To-yin Dania and Charlotte Ashamu remind me how sisterhoods move, travel, grow, and are glorious.

I am blessed to build and be supported by a wonderful team at The Armah Institute of Emotional Justice: Sena, Miriam, Adez, and Roger. You are so appreciated. We are a small and mighty team! To Diallo Shabazz, Madonna Kendona, and Georgina Lorencz—your guidance is so precious. To Rosalind McLymont—the idea of this whole institute started with you, and a lovely lunch at our Brooklyn fave, Jollof—a *thiebou dieun* to remember! I am forever grateful. To Gregory Reid, your legal mind helps us stay focused, and to Kate Gardiner, your expertise is so appreciated.

I am so grateful to my editor, Steve Piersanti, and the Berrett-Koehler Publishers family. Steve, you championed me and this book every step of the way. You are a blessing.

Index

About the Author

Esther A. Armah is a self-described global Black chick who claims three cities on three continents as home. Creative home = New York; birth home = London; spiritual and ancestral home = Accra. Each home is where she practiced journalism and wrote her plays, and each was a key contributor in developing the visionary Emotional Justice roadmap.

Armah is an international award-winning journalist who worked with the British Broadcasting Corporation (BBC) for ten years in London and was host of Pacifica Radio WBAI's *Wakeup Call* in New York. As founder and director of EAA Media Productions, she hosted and executive-produced *The Spin*, a podcast that aired online and on community radio stations in the US, Ghana, and Nigeria. From the mic to the stage, Armah has written five plays that have been produced and performed in New York, Chicago, and Accra, Ghana.

Globally, she has worked in London, New York, Washington DC, Chicago, Nigeria, Kenya, and South Africa. From journalist to teacher, Armah was a media communications lecturer with Webster University Ghana and the African University College of Communications (AUCC), and a commentator and consultant working with multiple media houses.

Armah's Emotional Justice essays have been published in books and other publications. They include the *New York Times* best seller *Four Hundred Souls: A Community History of African America 1619–2019*, coedited by Ibram X. Kendi and Keisha N. Blain; *Charleston Syllabus: Readings on Race, Racism, and Racial Violence*, coedited by Chad Williams, Kidada E. Williams, and Keisha N. Blain; and the award-winning *Love with Accountability: Digging Up the Roots of Child Sexual Abuse*, edited by Aishah Shahidah Simmons. Armah's Emotional Justice essays have been featured in publications including *WARSCAPES*, *Ebony.com*, *AlterNet*, *Essence.com*, *Gawker.com*, and *Jay Z's 4:44 Syllabus* by Anthony Boynton. The Emotional Justice roadmap was written about in the *Guardian*, and cited in the *New York Times* by critically acclaimed author Robert Jones Jr. as an inspiration for his book *The Prophets*.

Armah's work has led to her scooping awards in the US and Africa. For her Emotional Justice work, she won the Community Healer Award at the 2016 Valuing Black Lives Global

Emotional Emancipation Summit in Washington DC. Esther was named Most Valuable NY Radio Host in *The Nation*'s 2012 Progressive Honors List for her work on *Wakeup Call* on Pacifica's WBAI.

About The Armah Institute
of Emotional Justice

This global institute is the implementation home of the Emotional Justice roadmap. We do three things: projects, training, and thought leadership.

We introduce, apply, and implement the Emotional Justice roadmap in these three areas. The AIEJ projects are designed to introduce Emotional Justice to sectors as a change-agent roadmap that centers a practice of equity and empathy. The AIEJ trainings are designed to implement Emotional Justice in organizations and with leaders to make equity and racial healing sustainable practices. AIEJ thought leadership shows how Emotional Justice applies to topical issues as a reimagining of our world and a focus on a fuller humanity.

The AIEJ uses storytelling as a strategy for structural change. We privilege narrative and lead with equity and empathy, with collaboration as a central approach.

Training

The AIEJ researches, devises, designs, and develops flagship training that is then carefully shaped to work with each organization in each geographical region. Our training team includes artists, as we use storytelling within our training, and center narrative as a major tool for connection. The following are our flagship trainings:

* The Love Languages of Emotional Justice
* Introduction to Emotional Justice
* Emotional Justice Truth and Accountability Sessions
* Emotional Justice Consultation
* Circle of Willingness

The Love Languages of Emotional Justice

This three-part webinar explores the connection between labor, history, worth, and value for Black, Brown, and Indigenous women leaders and managers. It explores and answers the question, How do we institutionalize wellness, rest, and replenishment within the labor landscape of communities of color? This training introduces the Emotional Justice Equity Package. This training is specifically adapted to other demographics to explore reimagining a labor landscape that institutionalizes wellness.

This training is carefully adapted for two additional demographics: for white leaders in the philanthropic and nonprofit world, to explore their relationship to help and power, as part of a journey to centering an equity practice in this sector; and for white women leaders and managers, to develop a "circle of willingness" to chart a path of transformative change, actively engage resistance negotiation, and develop Emotional Justice as a working tool in their leadership arsenal.

Introduction to Emotional Justice

This is our online two-week course that introduces participants to the Emotional Justice roadmap in an interactive and creative way, with thought-provoking assignments.

Emotional Justice
Truth and Accountability Sessions

This three-part workshop followed by 3, 6, 9, or 12 months of facilitation is designed to create a sustainable equity practice within organizations by engaging our Emotional Justice roadmap to decenter whiteness and center Black, Brown, and Indigenous workers as an act of transforming organizational cultures. The post-workshop facilitation is designed to stand the workshop lessons and commitments on their feet and turn intention into outcome-focused equity.

Emotional Justice Consultation

We work with leaders of organizations in these two-part sessions to develop and engage them to devise Action Statements. Given that "public statements" pertaining to issues of race, racism, and racial healing are facing scrutiny and critique, Emotional Justice introduced the Action Statement; it is designed to center accountability, and requires leaders to be specific about the action they are taking to make change within their organization and/or sector.

Circle of Willingness

For white women leaders and managers where we explore their emotional work to unpack, identify, and explore their emotional relationship to whiteness and white masculinity, and how that impacts their power and shapes their leadership.

Projects

Our projects are creative and bold; they center storytelling and global Blackness and are devised to make racial healing a sustainable practice. Project examples include the following:

The Black Frontline

This is the world's largest oral history project of global Black doctors and nurses sharing their narratives and lived experience working with and navigating COVID-19. We gathered three hundred narratives from the US, the UK, and Ghana with a global team across those three nations to redefine a health care sector of the future that centers equity. The project's aim is to actively center those who are traditionally marginalized and to offer public health specialists, hospital administrators, and those studying medicine an active path to do this. The Black Frontline is codirected with Dr. Kim Gallon, founder of COVID Black. The narratives are published on the Black Frontline website, allowing public access, and a free curriculum guide is created to enable easy use. The Black Frontline's institutional home is Brown University in the US. The Black Frontline is a journey of sonic Blackness through the COVID-19 pandemic. It is developed through mixed methodologies and cross collaborations using oral history, journalism, data, and storytelling. It also draws on the theory and application of black digital humanities that, together with Emotional Justice, build an online world of stories, struggle, joy, pain, loss, grief, courage, community, and sacrifice.

Black Grief Matters

This is a three-part project exploring loss and grief through the lens of Black girls and women, as a path to create culturally competent curriculum for Social Emotional Learning educators in the US and the UK, with the goal of reducing suspensions and expulsions of Black girls. The three parts are the Creative Grief Journal, the Black Grief Matters Symposium, and the Black Grief Matters Online Modules Curriculum. The curriculum features case studies from the Creative Grief Journal, and excerpts from the talks delivered by academics, policymakers, and activists during the Symposium.

the STAYED and the STOLEN

This is an immersive experience bringing together Emotional Justice, digital humanities, and the world of gaming to create a transformative tour of the Cape Coast dungeons where enslaved Africans were held before being transported to North America, the Caribbean, Latin America, and Europe. This project focuses on intraracial healing among global Black people, centers Africa as a site of enslavement, and engages the digital to help humanize a dehumanized people.

Dear reader,

Thank you for picking up this book and welcome to the worldwide BK community! You're joining a special group of people who have come together to create positive change in their lives, organizations, and communities.

What's BK all about?

Our mission is to connect people and ideas to create a world that works for all.

Why? Our communities, organizations, and lives get bogged down by old paradigms of self-interest, exclusion, hierarchy, and privilege. But we believe that can change. That's why we seek the leading experts on these challenges—and share their actionable ideas with you.

A welcome gift

To help you get started, we'd like to offer you a **free copy** of one of our bestselling ebooks:

www.bkconnection.com/welcome

When you claim your **free ebook**, you'll also be subscribed to our blog.

Our freshest insights

Access the best new tools and ideas for leaders at all levels on our blog at ideas.bkconnection.com.

Sincerely,

Your friends at Berrett-Koehler

Certified

Corporation